Pageant of History

Nihilists

GENERAL EDITOR
John Gross

PAGEANT OF HISTORY SERIES

BANDITS—Eric Hobsbawm

DUELLING CORPS—Robert Baldick

GLADIATORS—Michael Grant

GURKHAS—David Bolt

HIGHWAYMEN—Christopher Hibbert

NIHILISTS—Ronald Hingley

THE SAINTS—Edith Simon

HITLER'S S. S.—Richard Grunberger

SAMURAI—Ivan Morris

Nihilists

Russian Radicals and Revolutionaries in the Reign of Alexander II (1855-81)

Ronald Hingley

Delacorte Press
NEW YORK

Originally published in England by
George Weidenfeld & Nicolson, Ltd.

LIBRARY OF CONGRESS CATALOG CARD NUMBER: 77-75097

Manufactured in The United States of America
First American Printing—April, 1969

TO

David Footman

Contents

Acknowledgements

The author and publishers are grateful for permission to reproduce the illustrations, the sources of which are given below. The illustrations taken from periodicals were photographed by John Freeman & Co. at the British Museum.

Graphic (1881), p. 110; *Gudok* (1862), p. 18 *below*; *Illustrated London News* (1880), pp. 62, 64, 106 *above*, (1881), pp. 68 *below*, 105 *above*, 108, 111, 112 *above*; Mansell Collection, pp. 17 *above*, 68, 70; Paul Popper Ltd, pp. 43 *below*, 44 *above*, 44 *below right*; Radio Times Hulton Picture Library, pp. 17 *below*, 41 *above*, 42 *below*, 43 *above*, 44 *below left*, 66, 105 *below*, 106 *below*, 107, 109 *above and below*; Royal Academy of Arts, p. 24 *above*; Society for Cultural Relations with the USSR, pp. 18 *above*, 19, 20 *above and below*, 21, 22, 23, 24 *below*, 42 *above*, 65, 67, 69; Staatsbibliothek, Berlin, pp. 41 *below*, 61 *above and below*, 63, 71 *above and below*, 72, 112 *below*.

Warmest thanks for their encouragement and criticism are due to my colleague Harry Willetts and to my wife; also to Mrs Olga Bowditch for secretarial help.

'The most terrifying reflection (I am speaking now for myself) is that all these people are not the product of the exceptional but of the general – of the normality of their place, and time, and race. The ferocity and imbecility of an autocratic rule rejecting all legality and in fact basing itself upon complete moral anarchism provokes the no less imbecile and atrocious answer of a purely Utopian revolutionism encompassing destruction by the first means to hand, in the strange conviction that a fundamental change of hearts must follow the downfall of any given human institutions. These people are unable to see that all they can effect is merely a change of names.'

JOSEPH CONRAD

(from the *Author's Note* to *Under Western Eyes*)

I

The New Men

A minor Nihilist, Vladimir Debogory-Mokriyevich, has recorded in his memoirs that 'actions, not words, count most in life - especially in the life of a revolutionary organization'.[1] If actions indeed speak louder than words, it may be as well to begin with the most spectacular *coup* of the Russian Nihilist movement, which took place on a dull Sunday afternoon in St Petersburg.

Shortly after two o'clock the Emperor Alexander II mounted his carriage near the centre of the city and was driven off down Engineer Street in the direction of his Winter Palace. Some of his predecessors had met sudden death, but it was not the fashion of Russian Tsars to slink about their capital unobtrusively, and the imperial carriage formed part of a small but dazzling cavalcade. The coachman was magnificent in his livery and short red cloak. An escort of fur-capped, scarlet-coated Cossacks, mounted on black horses and wearing silver daggers, led and flanked the carriage, which was followed at a short distance by two sleighs conveying the St Petersburg Chief of Police and other uniformed officers.

This ill-camouflaged cortège careered along at high speed to the T-junction with the Catherine Quay and turned right, now having the Catherine Canal on its left. Just over a hundred yards from the turning a nondescript youth threw a heavy object. It landed with a tremendous explosion under the back axle of the imperial carriage, but the carriage held together. The horses bolted and the coachman whipped them on; where one bomb had been thrown a second might easily follow. But the Tsar, who was unhurt, told him to pull up, dismounted and went back to the scene of the explosion, where the bomb-thrower had been seized by the police. A small crowd had collected. Chancing to hear an officer ask where he was, the Tsar said 'Thank God I am safe'.

He had walked a few steps back towards his carriage when another assassin, who had been leaning unnoticed against the railing by the Catherine Canal, threw a second bomb. It landed behind the Emperor at his feet. There was a great explosion, a whirl of smoke, snow and tumbling bodies, and when the first confusion subsided it was seen that the Tsar had been hurled back and was half sitting against the railing. His dark blue cloak and helmet had been blown off, his uniform was in shreds. Badly wounded in the legs, his face also covered with blood, he called weakly for help and complained of feeling cold, then insisted on being conveyed to the Winter Palace, where he died just over an hour later. His assassin, also fatally wounded, died on the same evening in hospital. There were three more deaths and some twenty other persons were injured.

Thus Alexander II died on 1 March 1881 in one of the most dramatic scenes of the century, with gorgeous uniforms and plunging horses set against the greys and blacks and dirty whites of the northern capital. The act was followed by another grim drama: the trial and public hanging of the killers. But what had happened? What was the significance of the sovereign's blood on the snow? And what were the main features of a reign which saw Russian Nihilism born as a fashion in clothing, manners and reading-matter, only to mature as revolutionary terrorism and reach its climax with the slaughter of the Autocrat?

It is hard to see the assassination in black-and-white terms. Alexander II was not a murderous tyrant struck down by the hand of avenging justice, any more than he was a liberal-minded statesman sacrificed to the blood-lust of psychopathic killers. His reign had begun with high hopes in 1855. After the oppressive atmosphere of Nicholas I's rule, the new accession brought an immediate feeling of relief, and the opening years of the reign were sometimes spoken of as a thaw: an image revived in Russia nearly a hundred years later to describe the change of climate after Stalin died. On each occasion the death of a tyrant allowed Russia to breathe more freely. Indeed, the departure of Nicholas I seemed to compensate for Russia's defeat in the Crimean War, which occurred in the following year. It was a moment of high morale and the weather seemed set fair. Alexander II at first encouraged such hopes by promoting long-needed reforms, of which the most important was the Emancipation of the Serfs in 1861. An overhaul of the legal system, of local government and of the armed forces followed in the next few years, but within a decade of his accession the Tsar's main reforming impetus was spent. In response to the growing revolutionary movement, reactionary ministers and officials tended to come to the fore, and there was a swing towards more oppressive policies: an evolution not uncommon in the history of rulers, whether in Russia or elsewhere.

There was no single dramatic turning point, but the situation had already begun to deteriorate in the year of Emancipation, 1861, which saw an increase in the local peasant riots so frequent in Russia. Many peasants thought the emancipation decree a fraud, and expected a second, 'real' emancipation which never came. Emancipation did free millions from slavery, but in many cases left them poorer than before. The year 1861 also saw the first serious student riots and the beginning of organized revolutionary conspiracy among Russian intellectuals. Later crises included the mysterious fires which terrified St Petersburg in 1862; Polish rebellion against Russian rule in 1863; the first attempted shooting of the Tsar by a Nihilist in 1866; the counter-revolutionary wave of the late 1860s called the White Terror; the attempts to foment peasant unrest in the 1870s; and the political assassinations of the years 1878–81.

It is easy to list these moments of mounting tension, but not so easy to see what went wrong. In general the government took measures strong enough to embitter the revolutionaries, but not ruthless enough to crush them. Official harshness provoked revolutionary violence and *vice versa*, making it hard to tell which side was the more to blame. The atmosphere became increasingly threatening as the authorities added the public hanging of revolutionaries to widespread imprisonment and exile, while the revolutionaries themselves graduated from propaganda to violence, terrorizing police chiefs, Governors General and the Emperor himself with revolver, dagger and dynamite: a process which found its consummation in the disaster on the Catherine Quay.

It was more as social curiosities than as potential assassins that Nihilists first appeared on the Russian scene, and it was not until several years had passed that they received that name, popularized in Turgenev's novel *Fathers and Children* (1862).

The New People (as they were also called) were mostly of humbler origin than the typical Russian intellectual of earlier generations, who tended to belong to the upper land-owning gentry. But the typical Nihilist did not come from the other end of the scale either, since not many were children of peasants, who formed the lowest and by far the largest Russian social class. Nihilists were mostly sons and daughters of poor gentry, of minor officials and of priests or lower clergy.

It was by external signs that the New People first attracted attention, one of these being their extreme youth: many began their activities while still at school. They had quirks of dress and manner, the men going about with huge beards and long hair flopping over their shoulders, while girls had their hair bobbed and renounced such frivolities as combs, crinolines and allowing men to kiss their hands. Both sexes favoured blue-tinted spectacles and high boots. Other common features were a heavy walking-stick and a rug flung over the shoulders in cold weather; they called it a plaid, but it was not necessarily a tartan. They were great cigarette smokers and were renowned for complexions of extreme pallor deriving from constant nervous strain and, it might be, spells in prison. Dirty, chewed fingernails, untidy clothes and an unwashed appearance were claimed by ill-wishers to be part of the style. Nihilists were also noted for the loudness of their voices and for the brusque or downright rude manner in which they spoke, generally to refute traditional beliefs in the sphere of religion, art and sexual morality, or to support materialism, utilitarianism, positivism and the study of science.

This was how they looked and sounded. But how did it feel to be a Nihilist? An intimate glimpse is given in the memoirs of Debogory-Mokriyevich, one of the most valuable Nihilist documents. He describes how, soon after leaving school in Kamenets Podolsk, he made a point of going back and parading in front of his former headmaster's window in a rig which aggressively contravened the school rules in every particular: he wore an unconventional shirt, high boots and blue glasses, and puffed furiously at a cigarette. ('I was delighted to see him [the headmaster] watching me through the window . . . and pretended not to recognize him.') One of the other masters, whom Mokriyevich later visited, 'looked at my long

The five Decembrist leaders hanged in 1826: Pestel, Ryleyev, Muravyov, Kakhovsky and Bestuzhev-Ryumin

Alexander Herzen (1812-70), leading émigré Russian political thinker

Contributors to *The Contemporary* (1856). Left to right: (seated) Goncharov, Turgenev, Druzhinin, Ostrovsky; (standing) Leo Tolstoy, Grigorovich

above opposite Michael Mikhaylov (1826–65), poet, propagandist of Nihilism and the first important political prisoner of Alexander II's reign

below opposite Michael Mikhaylov in prison

Chernyshevsky's 'civil execution' (drawing of 1863)

above opposite Nicholas Dobrolyubov (1836–61), leading radical critic and associate of Chernyshevsky

below opposite Dmitry Pisarev (1840–68), leading theoretician of early Nihilism

Nicholas Chernyshevsky (1828–89), main inspiration of Nihilism; author of *What is to be Done?*

Fyodor Dostoyevsky (1821–81), novelist; author of *Devils*

Ivan Turgenev (1818–83), novelist; author of *Fathers and Children*

Dmitry Karakozov (1840–66), first Nihilist to attempt to assassinate Alexander II

hair, blue spectacles and thick walking-stick, and said: "I can see you've drunk your fill of Nihilist wisdom". '[2]

From blue spectacles and long hair, Mokriyevich graduated, as was common, to full-time revolutionary activity. And, like other Nihilists when hunted by the police, he found it prudent later in life to dress less distinctively. The revelation came to him one day at a provincial railway station where an associate, a certain Lermontov, was being shadowed by the police: 'In one of the darker corners of the waiting room, Lermontov sat on a bench—but ye Gods, what a sight! Every fold of his clothing practically screamed "criminal" at you: the black felt hat on his head, the grey plaid on his shoulders and the blue spectacles on his nose! He was every inch the Nihilist and no mistake! "You won't get far in that rig," I thought, and on this, my first day as a member of the political underground, made a definite decision to comport myself quite differently.'[3]

Untidy youths who needed a haircut, murderers, assassins and dedicated revolutionary fanatics – all found their place among the Nihilists. Hooliganism and wanton minor destruction were not features of the movement; it was not public lavatories or the upholstery of railway carriages that they wanted to wreck, but society itself. Some, on the other hand, were merely engaged on an immemorial pastime of youth throughout the ages for which parallels can be found as far away as ancient Athens: shocking their elders. Besides those who perished on the scaffold, one must also remember those who eventually grew paunches, and who cut their hair or – depending on sex – grew it, becoming successful government officials, mothers of families, gold-prospectors, surgeons or oil tycoons; and in some instances also (for such is human nature) rabid anti-Nihilists.

Most Nihilists were university students at one time or another, but they often failed to graduate, since to leave or to be expelled before taking a degree was almost as much of a Nihilist diploma as having entered a university in the first place. Dmitry Karakozov provides an example of the Nihilist academic career *par excellence*. Before becoming the first person to attempt the assassination of Alexander II, in 1866, Karakozov achieved the distinction of being sent down from two universities: that of Kazan for taking part in student riots, and that of Moscow for not paying his fees. The terrorist leader Andrey Zhelyabov was a serf's son and an effective man of action not easily thought of as an intellectual. But he too contrived to attend a university, that of Odessa, before being expelled for taking part in a common student activity of the period: hounding an unpopular professor. Karakozov and Zhelyabov are only two among a host of Nihilists who were touched by higher education. And a Nihilist who had not at least attended a grammar school (*gimnaziya*) or school for sons of the clergy (*seminariya*) was quite a rarity, these establishments too being notorious centres of political opposition.

It is curious to note how many assassins worked as schoolmasters before exchanging chalk and blackboard for revolver or high explosive. Karakozov was a teacher for a time, as was Alexander Solovyov, who in 1878 repeated Karakozov's feat of trying to shoot the Tsar. The satanic Sergey Nechayev, chief ogre of the Nihilist movement, also did a stint as a master in a St Petersburg school, only to turn from moulding younger brains to blowing out older ones. And Sophia Perovsky took a schoolmistress's diploma long before she led the victorious Nihilist bomb-squad against the Emperor.

It has been well said that an intense faith in the beneficence of education was an article of the Nihilist creed.

Russian students had been rigidly regimented under Nicholas I, but when Alexander II came to the throne the new atmosphere made itself felt in the universities almost at once. Discipline was relaxed, the wearing of student uniform was stopped, and numbers expanded rapidly from an astonishingly low level: under three thousand throughout the whole Empire in 1853. Corporate student activities now became possible. And above all university gates were flung open to humbler entrants through a provision remitting academic fees for those who could not afford them. Now even the poorest young man could have a university education, provided of course that he could obtain a place. It was hard for him to earn the bare essentials of living by translating, copying, coaching schoolchildren and so on; but it was not impossible, besides which some student grants and scholarships were available.

To relax tyranny is often to provoke unrest, and these intellectual proletarians soon made it clear that they were not bursting with gratitude for their new opportunities: it was they who formed the liveliest recruiting base for Nihilism. The first student riots had begun in the provinces as early as 1856, but it was not until 1861 that they gained a real hold. There is not space to describe all the student disturbances of the period, and a better impression of them can be given by dwelling on one significant episode than by attempting to catalogue them all.

The year 1861 was a time of trouble for St Petersburg University. Early in the year the government tried to quell growing student unrest by making two bizarre new appointments in the educational field. Admiral Ye V. Putyatin became Minister of Education, and a General of Infantry, G. I. Filipson, was made Curator of the St Petersburg Educational District: a key post conferring control over all the state educational institutions within the area. Thus two elderly military men, with little if any educational experience, were brought in to give the students a taste of discipline. Soon afterwards reactionary regulations began to be introduced in St Petersburg University, suggesting that the government wanted to go back to the bad old days. Amongst other things free places for poor students were practically cancelled. The piecemeal introduction of the new measures was disconcerting too; wild rumours circulated, but no one could find out exactly what was intended.

Things came to a head at the beginning of the new academic year in September, when students began to hold protest meetings in empty lecture rooms. The authorities had them locked out, but they retaliated by breaking down the doors. They wanted a clear account of the new rules from General Filipson himself, but he would not see them, whether through diffidence or most unsoldierly cowardice in the face of an unfamiliar enemy.

On 25 September the students decided that if the General would not come to them, they must go to him. They marched *en masse*, nearly nine hundred strong, from the University over the River Neva and down the Nevsky Prospekt to his residence in Bell Street, a distance of about three miles. French barbers came out of their shops on the Nevsky to greet the procession and shouted '*Revolution! Revolution!*'[4] It had not quite come to that, but history was being made all the same: this was the first demonstration of the kind to have taken place in St Petersburg.

Arrived at General Filipson's residence, the students persuaded him to go back to the University with them almost as their prisoner, and to discuss their grievances with three delegates who were guaranteed immunity from arrest. But that night the delegates were arrested all the same, together with over a score of other students.

This did little to calm student feeling, and a number of clashes with the police, gendarmes (uniformed security police) and troops followed. According to accounts published in Herzen's *Bell*, there were about twenty cases of student demonstrators being struck by soldiers' rifle butts. One youth received a bayonet wound and another had his ear cut off by an over-zealous gendarme.[5] Several hundred students were arrested in all and put in the Peter and Paul Fortress or taken to the naval base at Cronstadt. They were not harshly treated in custody and most were released after a few weeks, but five ringleaders were sent into exile and the university was closed down for the rest of the academic year.

Other higher educational institutions in the capital and provinces showed solidarity with St Petersburg University, and henceforward student political demonstrations were an established tradition of the Empire. Though there was no more serious trouble in St Petersburg itself until 1869, the words 'student' and 'Nihilist' had now vaguely fused in people's minds as near-synonyms, while many of the academic liberties newly won in the years 1855–61 were eroded, suspended or cancelled.

Most students, and therefore most Nihilists, were atheists. Mokriyevich maintains that he did not know a single mature student at Kiev University who held religious beliefs, but it may well be that he equated the concepts mature and irreligious. In any case this attitude was not universal. For instance, Zhelyabov claimed under cross-examination at his trial that he 'accepted the essence of Jesus Christ's teaching', though he rejected Orthodox Christianity; he was repeating a common received idea of the period to the effect that Christ was the greatest revolutionary of them all. Karakozov, one of the more eccentric Nihilists, went further. He prefaced his assault on the Tsar with a pilgrimage to a monastery as well as with statements of an intention to commit suicide, and is said to have spent hours on his knees in passionate prayer before his execution. But this was far from typical, and many condemned Nihilists refused the ministrations of an Orthodox priest as offered to them on the scaffold.

On the whole an Orthodox Christian upbringing did not provoke anti-clerical militancy, but one prominent Nihilist of the 1860s, Vasily Sleptsov, was expelled from school for coming out with a confession of atheistic faith during the singing of the Creed in the middle of a church service. At the words 'I believe in one God', if the story is to be credited, he stepped forward on to the ambo and told the congregation that he himself believed in nothing of the sort.[6]

Freedom to travel abroad was one of many new relaxations enjoyed by Russian citizens under Alexander II, and one result of this was the establishment of student colonies in foreign towns, including Heidelberg and Zürich. Soon spies of the Third Section (Russian secret police) were reporting back that these places had been turned into cesspits of Nihilism. The area round the Zürich Polytechnic became heavily infested with young Russians whose loud voices and carefree gesticulations – not to mention their extreme Socialist views and reputation for promiscuity – shocked the staid burghers of that ancient Swiss city.

In the summer of 1873 the Russian government issued a decree ordering all female Russian students to quit Zürich on pain of being deprived of the right, which they had so far enjoyed, of sitting their examinations in Russia even if they might not study there. Many now came home accompanied by their young men, thus strengthening the revolutionary movement on Russian soil. As this shows, anti-Nihilist measures had an awkward way of backfiring on their authors.

2

Love in a Cold Climate

Nihilists of both sexes were much concerned about the 'woman problem', by which they meant female emancipation. They were not demanding votes for women. Men themselves had no vote except in certain minor local elections, so there was no question of a suffragette movement, nor was this an agitation about property rights. The main issues were careers and sexual freedom.

It was as a genteel spinster that the typical Nihilist girl entered adult life; in fact this was exactly what infuriated her. She would have preferred the chance to follow a profession instead of making a conventional marriage and settling down as a wife, mother and hostess. But institutions of higher learning were virtually closed to her, so how could she obtain the qualifications necessary for a career?

It is true that provisions began to be made for women to attend university courses in the late 1850s, and that liberal-minded professors were prepared to hold classes for them on private premises. But life was still difficult for the Russian blue-stocking. Facilities, limited in any case, varied from place to place and time to time; and female higher education was often the first casualty in the recurring gusts of political reaction, considered as it was to be a dangerously progressive phenomenon.

Another grievance was male legal control over a woman's passport, the misleading name for a document which was required for travel inside Russia as well as abroad. A father or husband could not quite put a refractory daughter or wife under house arrest, but he could legally stop her leaving the area in which he resided simply by refusing her a passport. To find that she could not go to St Petersburg or some other university city without male permission was understandably frustrating to a potential New Girl marooned in a provincial backwater; and even if she managed to obtain a passport, there were other obstacles ahead: not least the difficulty of finding respectable and congenial lodgings. The landladies of St Petersburg were notorious dragons; but then the average Nihilist young woman was well equipped to stand up for herself too. In fact the whole female emancipation movement was (one feels) unfair on Russian men, since in Russia the female of the species seems in general so much more redoubtable than the male.

Women were soon finding ways round the obstacles mentioned above. If her father refused her a passport, a girl might persuade or simply order some idealistic youth of the locality to marry her 'fictitiously'. There was nothing fictitious about the ceremony, which had to be a church wedding, the only kind of marriage possible under Russian law. The fiction lay in the motive, which was the emancipation of an individual female, and by no means the founding of a family: an institution much despised by Nihilists. Once married, the bride might briefly thank the groom for his services and vanish over the frontier with her new passport to Zürich, Heidelberg or some other foreign university where she could obtain instruction in chemistry and mathematics.

The thought of delicately-nurtured young ladies studying medicine, especially something as improper as anatomy, shocked old-fashioned parents, but it was a medical career that particularly attracted the girls themselves, and many decided to qualify as doctors at a time when there were few if any women-doctors in Western Europe. The best-known pioneer of medical studies for Russian girls was Nadezhda Suslov, who attended lectures at the Medical-Surgical Academy in St Petersburg until women were excluded in 1864. She then continued her studies at Zürich, receiving her medical diploma in 1868 – the first Russian woman to qualify in this way.

Women wanted sexual as well as professional freedom. Why should a wife remain faithful when her husband could run a string of mistresses without provoking more than a few raised eyebrows? Two could play at that game!

It was only one step from claiming such freedom as a theoretical right to the feeling that it was a sacred duty to exercise it in practice. This led the Nihilists into some ridiculous postures, for though there would be nothing remarkable in a licentious age adopting 'Thou shalt commit adultery' as its motto, the point is that this was not a licentious age. Far from it: the typical Nihilist, man or girl, had a strong puritanical streak. Anti-Nihilists might jeer at these young people as a bunch of libertines, whores or nymphomaniacs; but they were nothing so enterprising, erring as they did more on the side of prudishness than of promiscuity.

Once they had been shown the way, Russian girls often became more whole-heartedly Nihilist than the young men, but it was chiefly men who put the idea into their heads in the first place. And the men in turn often derived their inspiration from abroad. The Russian feminist movement was only part of the general European feminist movement of the nineteenth century, and Russian champions of female rights were well aware of what was going on outside their frontiers. For instance, the poet Michael Mikhaylov included a study of 'John Stuart Mill on Female Emancipation' in the series of influential articles on the woman problem which he published in the Russian radical journal *The Contemporary*. During a stay in Paris he met Jenny d'Héricourt, author of the militantly feminist work *La femme affranchie* (1860). But it was probably George Sand who became the best-known of Western feminists in Russia, and her novels influenced many Russian writers, including Turgenev, Dostoyevsky and Saltykov-Shchedrin.

Dmitry Pisarev, an important influence on the Russian feminist movement, started his short but brilliant career as a journalist working on *Dawn*, the first Russian woman's magazine, which began publication in 1859. His attitude to women was that of an orthodox Nihilist: wishing to marry his attractive cousin Raisa, he wrote to say that she should be at liberty to take lovers after marriage, since 'woman is free in spirit and body and can do what she likes with her life without accounting for herself to anyone, her husband included'. But Pisarev was stronger on theory than as a worker in the field. While he thus brooded on the privileges due to Raisa as his wife, she was quietly arranging to marry someone else. Pisarev was furious, and proceeded to waylay his rival at the Tsarskoye Selo Railway Station in St Petersburg – wearing a mask and offering to horsewhip him, according to one report. A fist fight followed and Pisarev was having the worst of it when the police came along and broke it up.

He later sent his successful rival an oracular challenge to a duel which came to nothing.

Pisarev behaved absurdly; but less so, surely, than those Nihilist husbands who pushed their wives into other men's arms in order to assert a principle. One of these was Nicholas Chernyshevsky, whose career as a feminist merits closer examination.

Chernyshevsky, who became the chief inspiration of Nihilism, began his work for women's rights by paying court to an attractive girl in his native Saratov. Even by Nihilist standards his style of wooing was grotesque. The flighty and vivacious Olga was accustomed to being pursued by gay young sparks of the locality, and must have been amazed to find herself now made the object of sociological experiment by an earnest suitor who addressed her as if she were a learned society in conclave.

Many of Chernyshevsky's harangues turned on the theory of female emancipation. Women had been so long subjected to men, he told her, that mere equality of the sexes was no longer enough. The scales must be tipped over in the opposite direction, not just balanced; in other words, there must in all fairness be a period when men would take their long overdue turn as underdogs. Chernyshevsky also explained that he intended to put his own future wife, whoever she might be, on a pedestal, remaining faithful and loyal while she should be free to run off with another man, bear his children and behave entirely as she wished.

Olga was used to a livelier conversational style; but as she half listened to Chernyshevsky's homilies, one salient point began to come through: there was something in this for her. She was unhappy at home, and here was a young man offering her a chance to shine in metropolitan society on a tolerable income while leaving her entirely her own mistress. It seemed like marriage without tears; which explains how the gayest and most sought-after marriageable girl in Saratov came to be captured by this bespectacled owl-like seminarist with his great braying laugh and elephantine style of banter.

It was not the first or last time that a pleasure-loving, frivolous girl has married a solemn scholar. The combination is by no means unworkable, but in this instance, perhaps, the gap was too wide. The scholar was over-solemn, and his young bride excessively pleasure-loving and frivolous; to the point, frankly, of being a thorough-going bitch, as evidence from several sources shows. A husband, to Olga, was just someone who bought her clothes and paid for her to visit theatre and opera, to attend fashionable balls and to keep good horses and a stylish carriage. After marriage, as before, young men continued to dance attendance on her, and this state of affairs continued for about nine years of married life preceding Chernyshevsky's arrest in 1862.

When he was held pending trial in the Peter and Paul Fortress in St Petersburg, Olga buried herself in the provinces. It was hard to persuade her to come to the city at all, and even when she did her first concerns were a shopping trip and an excursion to the opera, rather than a visit to her husband in the Fortress. She did later face the considerable ordeal of a journey to Chernyshevsky's prison in Siberia, though she showed no inclination to stay and share his fate: an act of devotion beyond the normal call of wifely duty, but common among the wives of Russian exiles and prisoners all the same. In any case he did not expect this; the wilds of Yakutia were not Olga's style at all, he was under no illusions about that.

Chernyshevsky's Siberian imprisonment drew on and on, while Olga's charms slowly faded. She neglected her young sons, became more and more concerned with imaginary illnesses and took to gadding about the country for no apparent reason. In later life she would harp on the indiscretions of her youth. It is not clear how systematically she had 'transgressed the bounds of ordinary flirtatiousness' (a delightful period phrase to cover marital infidelity). But she liked talking about such things – boasting, for example, of having been the mistress of a Polish *émigré* with whom, according to her account, she had misbehaved in an alcove while her husband was writing by a window in the same room. (Nothing in the character of either marriage-partner makes the story hard to believe.) She also spoke, on a more decorous level, of the time when she had taken part in an improvised horse race with the Grand Duke Constantine Nikolayevich, provocatively lowering her veil from time to time in order to 'pierce him with a fiery glance'.

All this was exactly what Chernyshevsky had – quite literally – asked for, and he seems to have been perfectly satisfied when his dream came true, even though other men might have found it more of a nightmare. He remained devoted to his wife and no complaint about her conduct is known to have crossed his lips. As the chief martyr of the radical movement, he has earned much sympathy; but one feels that Olga too is perhaps more to be pitied than despised.

To some extent, surely, her ugly postures were provoked by Chernyshevsky's door-mat complex, by his incitement of her to commit adultery before he had even brought her to the altar, and by the relish with which he savoured in advance his role of cuckolded husband.

The main interest of Chernyshevsky's love-life, and one reason for dwelling on it at such length, is that it so richly illustrates the common Nihilist tendency to regard human conduct, even in the most intimate personal relationships, as something subject to mechanical *a priori* regulation on the basis of abstract principles. The principles, like those of Tolstoy later, had the merit of extreme simplicity, and Chernyshevsky offered them to the youth of the 1860s with an air of bland superiority perhaps excusable because of the naïve eagerness with which the idea-hungry fledglings of the age snapped up each juicy worm. And he must be given full credit for consistency. Even a decade of married life with Olga Chernyshevsky did not stop him preaching his original brand of feminism in the pages of his novel *What is to be Done?* (1863).

This has been described with reason as the worst novel ever written, but to many Russians of the 1860s it was a sacred text, as well as a practical handbook of New Man's etiquette. It did more to mould the Nihilists' beliefs and influence their actions than any other single document.

The novel propagates Chernyshevsky's feminist views, as already outlined, in close combination with his cardinal ethical doctrine: the theory of rational egoism. It was his contention that human life could become a heaven on earth if only everyone would be selfish enough; but selfish in the right way. Thus a leader of the Russian revolutionary movement was to be found preaching in effect the virtues of private enterprise.

It is hard to square this teaching with Chernyshevsky's biography, since he himself seems to have had no jot of self-seeking in his make-up. Admittedly his whole career as the movement's great martyr can be interpreted as the indulgence of extreme masochistic urges, but he himself would have maintained that he was only following the dictates of higher self-interest in showing himself such a glutton for punishment. In any case, so far as selfishness in any normal sense is concerned, it was Olga Chernyshevsky who held the monopoly in that household.

In making his novel a sermon on rational egoism with special reference to the status of women, Chernyshevsky wrote a kind of wives' charter based on the principles which he had followed during his life with Olga. He dedicated the novel to her, but did not choose her as the model for his heroine. It was no use, after all, trying to cast Olga as a New Woman; for that role an idealized heroine, Vera, was called into being.

The action of the novel falls into two main parts, the first of which deals with Vera's escape from the world of middle-class St Petersburg. Her liberator, a poor medical student called Lopukhov, is visiting tutor to her younger brother. The presence of a personable but ineligible young man in the house at first disturbs Vera's calculating mother, who has her eye on a rich young officer as her future son-in-law. But close observation shows her that Lopukhov never casts a single lascivious glance at her daughter, regarding her instead with a gaze 'purer than that with which many a brother looks at his sister'. Far from indulging in any hanky-panky, he only seems interested in lending her books by such dull-sounding writers as Victor Considérant and Ludwig Feuerbach. Nothing could have been more sinister in fact; but not to Vera's mother, who knew nothing of the style of wooing practised by the New People and had never heard of the authors concerned anyway. She little dreamed that her daughter was pioneering the classical escape-route for Nihilist girls stifled by domestic tyranny, later to be described by the critic Nestor Kotlyarevsky as: 'Firstly a book, but one not recommended by her family or school; and secondly the young man who brings her the book.'[7]

Secretly married to Lopukhov, Vera leaves the hell of lower-middle-class St Petersburg for the heaven of rational egoism as practised by the New People. She takes the initiative in laying down the house rules of marriage *à la* Chernyshevsky, and it is at her suggestion that she and Lopukhov divide up the three rooms of their rented flat into his, hers and neutral, agreeing never to intrude uninvited on each other's territory or private life. About five months after the marriage she begins to show signs of a mysterious change of mood, and coyly announces that she has a secret to confide. This turns out to concern nothing so banal as the patter of tiny feet; she is pregnant with a brain-child: a co-operative dressmaking establishment to be set up on a profit-sharing basis. Lopukhov is so delighted with the idea that he insists on breaking Nihilist convention by kissing her hands, and the new dressmaking establishment is soon a going concern.

From now on the main theme in Vera's story is the development of a triangular love situation and its solution in the style of the New People. It turns out that Lopukhov's friend and former fellow-student Kirsanov is in love with Vera, and she with him. The two men are both portrayed as such monumental prigs that it is not clear why Vera should prefer one to the other, or even how she can tell them apart, but the transfer is engineered with great delicacy over several score pages, all three parties trying to act on the basis of rational egoism.

It seems likely that Chernyshevsky modelled much of his novel on the experiences of an acquaintance, Mary Obruchev, who followed an orthodox Nihilist career. She was, with Nadezhda Suslov, one of the first Russian girls to study medicine, and in order to do so she 'fictitiously' married a young medical student. The marriage, as in *What is to be Done?*, became a real one for a time, after which a change of partners was amicably negotiated and she lived happily in 'civil matrimony' with a well-known professor of physiology: all very much on the lines of Chernyshevsky's novel.

Such accommodations were typical of the period. 'Never in Russia had there been so many wives and husbands living apart as in and after the 1860s [one writer, Nicholas Shelgunov, records with satisfaction]. Unsuccessful families split up and then formed new families, which were illegal, and society inevitably treated these new, illegal families with complete tolerance. The question whether a woman was someone's legal wife or not became impossible and meaningless.'[8] This was true, but somewhat exaggerated; readers of Tolstoy's *Anna Karenin*, set in Russia of the 1870s, will receive a different impression.

Shelgunov, whose memoirs have just been quoted, was a typical Nihilist husband in showing himself ready (if one may be forgiven the expression) to lay down his wife for his friend. The friend in question has already figured in this sketch: Michael Mikhaylov, poet and pioneer of Russian women's rights. In 1861 Mikhaylov was arrested in the apartment which he shared with the Shelgunovs, for writing and distributing subversive proclamations, and was then tried and sentenced to penal servitude in Siberia. Soon after he had left, Shelgunov persuaded his wife Lyudmila that they should both go to Siberia to join Mikhaylov. There were many precedents for wives following their husbands into exile, but it took a Nihilist husband to convey his wife several thousand miles into the heart of Siberia so that she could be reunited with her lover; it is also true that they were hoping to arrange his escape.

By no means all Russians of the period lacked a sense of the ridiculous, and one minor writer, Nicholas Shcherbina, saw the funny side of this affair. He questioned Lyudmila Shelgunov's motives in agreeing to go to Siberia. According to him publicity was the lure, not her lover, and he said that she hoped to be immortalized in some French encyclopaedia with the entry '*Schelgounoff, Madame de, la première agitatrice politique russe*'. Lyudmila, a girl of spirit, repaid him in kind in her memoirs when she called him a bloated, bilious little man with a red face who bored everyone by constantly coining tiresome epigrams.[9]

The supreme baiter of Nihilists was Dostoyevsky, whose five last novels are all to some extent the product of a violent reaction against the movement and above all against the theory of rational egoism. The Nihilists, none more than Chernyshevsky, incensed the great novelist, driving him into spasms of creative frenzy such as he had never enjoyed before they stung him into hitting back. Their habit of committing adultery as a matter of solemn duty particularly provoked him. One of his Nihilists, Lebezyatnikov in *Crime and Punishment*, is made to say that if he ever married he would not merely allow his wife to have a lover, but would insist on it: 'I love you, darling, but I also want you to respect me.' Dostoyevsky liked this joke so much that he repeated it in his novel *Devils* (1871–2; better known in translation as *The Possessed*). Here one of his Nihilists celebrates his wife's taking a lover with the comment: 'My dear, hitherto I had only loved you. Now I respect you.'

One important topic in *What is to be Done?* is the dressmaking cooperative set up by Vera Lopukhov, which eventually blossoms into a self-supporting commune. This inspired Nihilists of the period to set up their own communes on similar lines, though when one tries to track down these enterprises the evidence seems elusive.

The best-documented commune is that established on Znamensky Street in St Petersburg by Vasily Sleptsov in 1863–4. There is much conflicting evidence about this, but on one point all authorities seem agreed: Sleptsov was a charming young man with whom girls,

Nihilist and non-Nihilist, all too easily fell in love. But he was also a serious feminist, doing everything he could to help women who came to St Petersburg with eager aspirations but no visible means of support. He found work for them as translators, copyists, bookbinders and so on; organized courses in popular science for them on private premises; and helped to solve their housing problem by establishing his commune. But it seems to have been more of a hostel than a business enterprise, so the parallel with Vera Lopukhov's dressmaking co-operative breaks down.

Sleptsov's place was no Nihilist 'pad'. In fact some accounts describe it as an exceptionally lavish apartment complete with uniformed commissionnaire and extravagant catering arrangements. Another version has it that only tea was offered to the numerous guests – but in quantity, the drinking of tea being a great preoccupation of the Nihilists, as of Russians in general. They were apt to speak of it with an air of guilt such as would not have been assumed when referring to vodka, which in any case was avoided by the more puritanical Nihilists. Tea was expensive (in *What is to be Done?* the Lopukhovs reckoned to spend ten roubles a month on it, a third as much as the rent of their flat) and, from the prominence given to it in Nihilist memoirs, seems to have been their great form of self-indulgence both inside and outside gaol. Michael Mikhaylov's splendid account of prison life has much to say about it, and Dostoyevsky's Nihilist Kirillov, in *Devils*, will be remembered as a compulsive tea-drinker.

The tea-drinking orgies in Sleptsov's commune gave rise to wild rumours in the neighbourhood. Perhaps more than tea-drinking was involved? Did Sleptsov and his tenants belong to some weird Russian religious sect of the kind known to indulge in promiscuous orgies? This idea was widely mooted among the neighbours, who had also noted that the regular members of the commune were all women except for Sleptsov and one friend. In the end the commune fell apart because some of the girls were not Nihilist-minded enough and objected to being compromised. The aristocratic and 'beatnik' elements among them were at daggers drawn anyway, and the place had attracted the attention of the police, quite apart from the mundane consideration that they could not pay their bills.

3

Unholy Writ

Nihilist reading-matter plays a crucial part in the story. It was especially important in a country so open to literary influence that many individuals would decide to remodel their whole lives after perusing a single poem, novel or work of political philosophy.

Nihilist theory was a vague assortment of ideas, not a coherent body of doctrine, and like much else in Russian thought it ultimately derived from the West. Western European political, philosophical and scientific sources of Nihilism include Louis Blanc, Comte, Darwin, Fourier, Lassalle, John Stuart Mill, Robert Owen, Saint-Simon and Herbert Spencer; and also the English historian Henry Buckle, who enjoyed a great vogue, as did a trio of forgotten German materialists, Büchner, Moleschott and Vogt.

Important as these influences were, it was their Russian exponents and interpreters who really moulded the movement and provided its most significant texts: often works of imaginative literature. In Turgenev's novel *Fathers and Children* (1862) the word Nihilist, which has a complicated earlier history, was (in effect) first attached as a label to the Russian New People. The name caught on at once, no doubt because Bazarov, the Nihilist hero of the novel, is so vividly portrayed.

A Nihilist (Bazarov's disciple Arkady explains) 'does not bow down before any authority, and accepts no principles on trust, however much respect they may enjoy'. Bazarov despises all abstract thought, together with the romantic and idealistic postures typical of the older generation. He is a materialist – though he scorns to go round preaching materialism, or indeed anything else – and believes in science. ('A decent chemist is twenty times more useful than any poet.')

Michael Bakunin (1814–76), leading anarchist

Bakunin's cell in the Peter and Paul Fortress, St Petersburg

above opposite Prince Peter Kropotkin (1842–1921), the well-known anarchist, in 1864

below opposite A later photograph of Prince Peter Kropotkin

left Peter Lavrov (1823–1900), leading thinker and influence on the Populists

below Vera Zasulich (1849–1919), who attempted to assassinate General Trepov

top Count Michael Loris-Melikov (1825-88), a prominent figure in the movement to suppress the Nihilists
above left Vera Figner (1852-1942), leading terrorist and memoirist of the period
above right Vera Figner in old age, the grand old lady of Nihilism

This anti-aesthetic attitude is another characteristic of the Nihilists, who tended to judge a work of art solely on the basis of its usefulness, the classic formulation of their view-point being Chernyshevsky's *Aesthetic Relations of Art and Reality* (1855). Chernyshevsky's thesis is expressed somewhat more pithily in a common saying of the period: that a good pair of boots was worth more than the entire works of Pushkin. So when Arkady's father is found reading Pushkin, Bazarov arranges for the volume to be taken off him and for a substitute to be tactfully offered – not a pair of boots, but something almost as indigestible: Büchner's treatise *Stoff und Kraft*.

Bazarov is not the complete Nihilist. He is heretical in his attitude to the woman problem, being off-hand, cynical and frankly less interested in a woman's theoretical potentialities than in her attractiveness. He bluntly states that if you take a fancy to a girl you should go ahead and get what you want out of her, but not long after parading this no-nonsense attitude he falls hopelessly and tragically in love, showing himself more a Young Werther than a New Man. Then he perishes in one of the best-known death-bed sequences in Russian literature, after accidentally infecting himself with typhus. Whatever Turgenev's conscious intention, this emphasis on death and sentimental love has the practical effect of diminishing the stature of his gruff man of action. And is Bazarov, after all, a man of action? He is well characterized as such, but what action does he ever take? Not much, it seems, beyond the occasional collecting and dissecting of frogs.

Partly because of censorship, Turgenev left other gaps in his hero's equipment. To be the complete Nihilist, Bazarov would have to be an atheist, something which Turgenev does not state outright, though he does manage to drop at least one broad hint in that direction. Still less could Turgenev state in so many words that Bazarov was a revolutionary. That he conceived him as such is explicitly declared in a letter of 26 April 1862: Turgenev's reaction to a sort of field court-martial held by Russian Nihilist students in Heidelberg to condemn *Fathers and Children* as a libel on the younger generation. It is characteristic of the man that he should have thrown himself on the mercy of these self-appointed judges. Sycophantic truckling to such impudent juveniles was one of the accusations later levelled against Turgenev when Dostoyevsky lampooned him (as the 'great writer' Karmazinov) in his novel *Devils*. As for Dostoyevsky himself, he was quite indifferent to what any Nihilist might think about him.

Turgenev also fared badly with the older generation, who objected to the respect accorded in *Fathers and Children* to the wretched Bazarov, before whom (they claimed) he crawled in self-abasement. Turgenev came to feel that he had ruined his reputation for life by writing the novel. He paid the penalty of trying to be fair to both sides in an age of growing intolerance, though representatives of each political extreme were found to support him. The radical thinker Dmitry Pisarev became a great patron of Bazarov, of which more will be said later. At the other end of the scale the Third Section gave Bazarov an unsolicited testimonial in a report to the Tsar on Russian activities in the year 1862: 'Turgenev has branded our adolescent revolutionaries with the corrosive name Nihilist and has shaken the doctrine of materialism and its representatives.'[10]

A fine novel, *Fathers and Children* did not deserve the ultimate insult of being acclaimed by the imperial secret police, but it remains the tamest of the great Nihilist texts. Turgenev's attitude is altogether too indecisive, as can be seen by comparing his novel with Dostoyevsky's *Devils*, the greatest work of imaginative literature devoted to Nihilism. The fact is that the arch-scourge of Nihilists was temperamentally closer to his subject than was Turgenev. Turgenev did his best to understand Nihilism, Dostoyevsky was more concerned to crush it. But he brought to the process of demolition a ferocity matching that of the Nihilists themselves, so that he and his Nihilists are real brothers under the skin, which can hardly be said of Turgenev and Bazarov. But then Dostoyevsky had himself been a sort of Nihilist *avant la lettre* in the 1840s and was cauterizing the sins of his own youth.

Devils was by no means the only specimen of a novel directed against Nihilism. In the 1860s and 1870s the pages of Russian periodicals became flooded with anti-Nihilist fiction, the chief authors concerned being Nicholas Leskov, Vsevolod Krestovsky, Aleksey Pisemsky and Victor Klyushnikov. There is unfortunately not space to discuss these works here, but they have been well analysed in Mr Moser's valuable study, *Antinihilism in the Russian Novel of the 1860s*.[11]

From a literary point of view all the big guns were on the anti-Nihilist side, especially if one accepts Moser's classification of

Fathers and Children as anti-Nihilist. To pit Dostoyevsky, Turgenev and Leskov against Chernyshevsky in the battle of the novels is like ranging a battery of howitzers against a pea-shooter. What makes the line-up even more unfair is that the anti-Nihilists enjoyed greater freedom from censorship, being more in tune with official government policy. They could roundly denounce revolution, while the revolutionaries could barely hint at the existence of such a thing. However, as already indicated, it was not Dostoyevsky's *Devils*, and still less Pisemsky's *Troubled Sea* or Klyushnikov's *Mirage* which fired the imagination of the young, but Chernyshevsky's *What is to be Done?*

Some aspects of Chernyshevsky's novel have already been discussed. It now remains to mention its most influential character, Rakhmetov, who plays only an incidental role and is brought in by way of digression, yet is the real hero.

This athletic saint has just the right academic background, having attended university – but without finishing his course. He happens to be rich, but gives nearly all his money away. He systematically hardens himself by doing gymnastics and tough physical work, lives on a worker's frugal fare or on a boxer's diet of nearly raw beef; avoids alcohol and women; refuses to sleep with a blanket or mattress; never wastes time. In a marathon bout of reading lasting eighty-two hours he has sucked the essence of European political thought out of a stack of books bought at one of the French or German bookshops in St Petersburg. In another fit of wilful martyrdom he once equipped himself with an ointment 'for healing wounds from sharp weapons', then proceeded to spend the night on a bed of nails, from which he arose in bloodstained underwear, having proved his powers of physical endurance. Like many heroes of Soviet novels ultimately inspired by him, he is allowed a single weakness to emphasize his humanity: smoking cigars.

For reasons of censorship this weird superman could not be portrayed as a fully-fledged revolutionary, but the pulsations of revolutionary militancy emanate from him much more noticeably than they do from Turgenev's Bazarov. Besides, who would dream of imitating Bazarov? It could only mean striking a pose, whereas Rakhmetov offered a detailed pattern of behaviour on which (excluding the bed of nails) many Nihilists were able to model their daily lives. So in turning from *Fathers and Children* to *What is to be Done?*

the reader was moving from a politically tame work of acknowledged literary merit to a bad novel with inflammatory political implications, and from a 'safe' writer to a risky one.

The fact that Chernyshevsky's Nihilist Bible could openly appear on the pages of a journal subject to censorship may seem puzzling, and it becomes more so if one takes into account the circumstances in which the writing was done: in solitary confinement in a cell of the Peter and Paul Fortress in St Petersburg. Chernyshevsky was still there awaiting trial for political crimes when, in early 1863, his novel was being serialized in *The Contemporary*.

The fact is that someone had blundered. Before reaching the ordinary censor's office the text had been submitted to special pre-censorship devoted solely to considering whether or not it contained material prejudicial to the trial. This was carried out by an exalted Investigating Commission of the Senate, which signified its approval and then handed the manuscript on for submission to the regular censorship. Seeing the stamp of approval imposed by a body so august, the ordinary censor passed it without more ado. He was later dismissed from his post, but by that time *What is to be Done?* was catching on. Copies in book form were not available, but the relevant volumes of *The Contemporary* were bound together and changed hands for as much as twenty-five roubles: a fantastic price to pay for a bad novel.

The Contemporary had become the great radical journal of the period, but it had a keen rival in *Russian Word*, the organ of Dmitry Pisarev. There were marked differences of emphasis between the two publications, and one of these lay in Pisarev's readiness to accept the label Nihilism as applying to his own doctrines. He did not quite go so far as to proclaim himself a Nihilist, the term which he preferred being Realist, but he was the only notable thinker to associate himself so enthusiastically with Turgenev's Bazarov as a spokesman of the younger generation. 'Whoever,' Pisarev wrote, 'has once in his life, if only for a few minutes, looked at things with the eyes of a Bazarov – such a person remains a Nihilist all his life.' Pisarev himself looked at things repeatedly through the eyes of a Bazarov over several years, and after devoting more printed words to explaining Bazarov than had his original creator, began to feel that he had acquired proprietary rights.

Turgenev had portrayed his Nihilist hero as a sympathetic figure, but that was not enough for Pisarev, who increasingly sought to explain away such flaws in Bazarov's character as rudeness and occasional cruelty. Bazarov had to be canonized as a Nihilist saint, which reminds one of yet another Nihilist trait: there was nothing that these iconoclasts so craved as new icons before which to bow down. No sooner had a priest's son thrown off his ancestral faith than he was busily casting around for some new secular religion to take its place. Not that Pisarev himself was the son of a priest; he was born a gentleman; but, as many instances show, this apparent disadvantage need be no obstacle to a successful Nihilist career.

Bazarov is, in a sense, the original Nihilist, and Pisarev became his chief prophet, so one might expect to discover the ultimate essence of Nihilism distilled in Pisarev's long glosses on *Fathers and Children*. To some extent this is so. Pisarev was a materialist, a utilitarian, a believer in progress and an advocate of science – being at one in all these features with the typical Nihilist, as also in his rejection of established authority. His own contribution to the philosophy of the movement lay chiefly in the distinction which he drew between the *élite* of what he termed Realists and the broad masses of those who never use their brains, but follow others like sheep. He was thus far removed from the teaching of those, later to be called Populists, who sought to identify themselves with the masses. This and some more trivial issues led to an embittered quarrel between *The Contemporary* and *Russian Word* in 1864–5, at a time when Russian radicals might have been better advised to join forces than to tear each other in pieces. But it was an age of polemical violence when anyone who offered a rival interpretation of Bazarov or Rakhmetov must be pilloried as an intellectual, moral and physical cripple.

It was only for a brief period in 1862 that Pisarev advocated revolutionary views, a point which detracts from his credentials as a Nihilist as the word is understood in the present study. Nor would he cultivate a Nihilist style, being unusually neat in appearance. How flagrantly he defied convention in this particular is shown by a passage from Turgenev's correspondence: 'The main thing is – *il* [Pisarev] *a l'air d'un enfant de bonne maison*, as they say; he has beautiful hands *and nails of the proper length* [italics added], which is a little strange for a Nihilist.'[12]

The Nihilist texts so far discussed were openly published in the

Russian press after being passed by the censor, but there was also a steady flow of illicit material, large quantities of which were smuggled in from abroad or printed in Russia itself on secret presses. It was this sort of literature that gendarmes first looked for when they raided a Nihilist hideout. There was a great profusion and variety of it throughout the period, culminating in the triumphant broadsheet which came off the press of *People's Will* on 2 March 1881 to announce the assassination of Alexander II. But it is the earlier material which must now be briefly considered, together with the fate of some of the authors concerned.

Alexander Herzen, who emigrated from Russia in 1847 and settled in Western Europe, was an important source of such contraband, together with his collaborator Nicholas Ogaryov. Herzen set up his Free Russian Press in London in 1853. Its publications included books and manifestoes, the review *Polar Star* (1855–62 and 1869) and – most influential item – the periodical called *The Bell*, which appeared monthly or fortnightly between 1857 and 1867. *The Bell* was regularly smuggled into Russia, where it is said to have had a circulation of two thousand five hundred: a respectable total even when compared with the figures for legally published reviews of the time. *The Bell* was probably read by Alexander II himself, as he could find in it information on abuses such as was not likely to reach him through normal channels.

Among many other items, the Free Russian Press printed the manifesto *To the Younger Generation* (1861) written by Nicholas Shelgunov, with some assistance from Michael Mikhaylov, who smuggled six hundred copies into Russia in a trunk with a false bottom. The manifesto was posted in public places, despatched through the mail and even – according to one report – broadcast along the Nevsky Prospekt in St Petersburg by a daredevil rider on a galloping horse. It called for the overthrow of the Tsar and his replacement by a salaried official, as also for land reform, free speech and elections.

The episode led to the first political trial of importance during Alexander II's reign. Betrayed by an associate, Mikhaylov took more than his share of the responsibility for *To the Younger Generation*, in order to save Shelgunov and Lyudmila Shelgunov, who (as mentioned earlier) happened to be Mikhaylov's mistress. He was sentenced to twelve and a half years' penal servitude in Siberia, to be followed by permanent exile, the period of penal servitude being reduced to six years by the Tsar, who reviewed all such sentences and often changed them.

Mikhaylov's trial was made the occasion to revive for political offenders the grotesque ceremony called 'civil execution', to which many other victims were subjected later in Alexander II's reign. On a scaffold specially erected in public, the culprit was chained to a 'pillar of shame' and forced to kneel while a sword was ceremonially broken over his head. His sentence was solemnly read out in the hearing of the crowd and of a military and police escort. The idea was to hold the victim up to public execration, but the effect was often to gain sympathy. Contrary to official hopes, it was flowers rather than rotten eggs which tended to be thrown, though such demonstrations themselves involved risk of arrest.

Mikhaylov was taken to Siberia by carriage with the regulation chain and fetters attached to his ankles and under the armed escort of two amiable gendarmes. Rumours of a plot by a posse of armed students to rescue him near the capital led to special security precautions being taken, but the story proved unfounded.

It is a measure of political feeling at the time that Mikhaylov was received in Tobolsk in Western Siberia as the hero of the hour, being the first Russian political prisoner to have been sentenced to penal servitude under Alexander II. Mikhaylov's fetters were struck off and he was showered by the cream of local society with invitations to dinners which he was allowed to attend, though confined in the town gaol. Those responsible for treating him as a conquering hero were later brought before a special tribunal and condemned, and Mikhaylov himself, whose health was not very good, perished in a remote settlement on the Chinese frontier in 1865, after contributing some exhilarating pages to the large corpus of Nihilist memoirs.

To the Younger Generation was only one among many clandestine manifestoes of the period. An especially violent specimen was *Young Russia*, the work of a student, P. G. Zaichnevsky, who ran a small secret printing-press in Moscow for about three years. Zaichnevsky was one of the least security-conscious of Nihilists and his open preaching of Socialism led to his arrest in 1861.

The text of *Young Russia* was, amazingly, concocted in a Moscow prison, and smuggled out with the connivance of a warder, after the author had succeeded in converting his cell into a sort of club which fellow-students could visit at will. The manifesto calls for a revolution, bloody and merciless, in which rivers of blood would flow while many innocent people would perish. As for the imperial family, it must be exterminated.

The use of a prison cell as a revolutionary headquarters, the fêting of a 'political criminal' in Siberia and the scattering of forbidden leaflets from a galloping horse in St Petersburg's main thoroughfare – these are all details emphasizing a certain carefree and easy-going atmosphere in Alexander II's Russia. At times one tends to forget that the story of the Nihilists, and of the sufferings which they courted and inflicted, was in fact a sombre affair.

Chernyshevsky's grim fate brings this home. He was accused at his trial of communicating with Herzen and of wishing to subvert the existing order. A more specific charge, that of composing a manifesto addressed to the peasants, was probably based on faked evidence. The trial was, in fact, very much a frame-up, though the exact extent of Chernyshevsky's involvement in any specific conspiracy is still disputed. In any case his real offence was his influence on young people through *What is to be Done?*, so that he was in the unusual position of having committed his chief crime while already in custody. He was sentenced to fourteen years' penal servitude, later commuted to seven, to be followed by permanent exile to Siberia. On 19 May 1864 he was 'civilly executed' in public, and submitted to the indignity with great nonchalance, according to eyewitness report. Soon afterwards he was despatched to Siberia under the customary escort of two gendarmes, his ankles fettered in accordance with regulations. Nearly twenty-five years of penal servitude and exile followed.

Pisarev's was the third notable literary-political trial of the early 1860s. He spent four and a half years (1863–7) in the Peter and Paul Fortress for writing an article (which had not been published) attacking Alexander II as a tyrant in the style of Nicholas I. It was in prison that Pisarev produced his most influential work. The period comprised about half his working life; he was drowned at the age of twenty-seven, in the year following his release. His great influence and that of Nicholas Dobrolyubov, who died in 1861 at an even earlier age, remind one how much the Nihilist movement was dominated by the young. Even Chernyshevsky, the grand old man of Nihilism, was only thirty-four when he wrote *What is to be Done?*

4

Conspirators of the 1860s

The suppression of the Decembrists, after their attempted *coup* at the time of Nicholas I's accession in 1825, had led to a decline in Russian revolutionary activity. Now, in the early 1860s, the tradition was revived with the formation of the first political secret society on any considerable scale for some three and a half decades: *Land and Freedom.*

It is important not to confuse this movement with the other secret society bearing the same name and active in the late 1870s. The first *Land and Freedom* attracted less attention than its later namesake, but it was a fairly elaborate organization with branches in the provinces as well as in Moscow and St Petersburg. It looked to Chernyshevsky as inspiring genius rather than conspiratorial leader, the two most active members being brothers: Nicholas and Alexander Serno-Solovyevich. The younger, Alexander, has already figured anonymously in this narrative, as the intrepid horseman who galloped down the Nevsky Prospekt scattering copies of the manifesto *To the Younger Generation.* The elder brother was also adventurously disposed; he once accosted the Tsar in the grounds of his palace at Tsarskoye Selo and handed him a manuscript designed to convert him to Socialism.

Land and Freedom represented a reaction to the Emancipation of the Serfs in 1861: a feeling that the personal freedom granted to the peasants was not enough, but that they should also be given land free of charge, instead of having to make the crippling redemption payments imposed upon them together with their liberty.

The society also sought political liberty for the Empire as a whole, including permission for minority nationalities to secede from Russia. This led the conspirators to support Polish rebellion against

Russian rule in 1863. But though *Land and Freedom* drew up an agreement with the Polish rebels, it was unable to give effective help. Some Polish conspirators tried to make use of Russian Nihilist students at Kazan on the middle Volga to provoke a peasant revolt in the heart of Russia, calculating that such a diversion would help their own struggle in the Polish homeland. It was a forlorn hope. They did prevail on a Moscow member of *Land and Freedom* to draw up a false manifesto to the Kazan peasants in the name of the Tsar, a classic Nihilist device for starting rural riots. But the plot collapsed when the main Polish conspirators were caught and executed. As for *Land and Freedom*, it too collapsed, and had ceased to have any effective existence by the end of 1863.

It was not easy in any case for Russian revolutionary champions of peasant welfare to make common cause with a Polish nationalist movement dominated by priests and led by aristocratic landowning patriots more easily thought of as exploiters than as liberators of their own peasants. Besides, there was something about Poles which made the most internationally-minded Russian tend to forget the brotherhood of man: an attitude which the Poles, for their part, returned with interest.

Thus the Polish freedom movement was not popular with Russian Nihilists, in spite of the support lent to it by *Land and Freedom*. One important Russian oppositionist, Herzen, did support the Poles, but this very fact contributed to the rapid decline of his influence over the revolutionary movement: a decline which dates from 1863. There was also a clash of temperament between Herzen and his younger compatriots. Here was this Russian gentleman luxuriating (they thought) among the flesh-pots of London while others faced death or exile to Siberia. Besides, he refused to hand over to his Nihilist visitors in London the money which they vociferously demanded for the cause, and which he could less easily afford than they imagined. The dislike was mutual. To Herzen many of these young Nihilists were scruffy, ill-bred, semi-delinquent scroungers.

New and more exotic conspiracies took the place of *Land and Freedom*. One of these is of special importance because it gave rise to the first attempt to assassinate the Tsar. Called simply *The Organization*, it had its main centre in Moscow and was linked with a similar group in St Petersburg. The movement marks a further stage in Chernyshevsky's evolution as patron saint of Nihilism. Its leader, Nicholas Ishutin, regarded the martyr of Saratov as one of the three greatest men in history, and the identity of his other two candidates is of interest: Christ and St Paul. Chernyshevsky's Rakhmetov was the model for *The Organization*; its members led ascetic lives, often slept on the floor and gave all their money – some were quite well off – to the cause. Many abandoned university studies to organize co-operative workshops. They started a boys' school in a Moscow slum in order to train revolutionary disciples, and also hatched various criminal schemes to raise revolutionary funds – planning, for example, a mail-coach robbery. One member was prepared to poison his father and give his inheritance to the cause, a plot which went far enough to lead to his prosecution and exile.

There was also created, within *The Organization* itself, a special nucleus called *Hell* for purposes of political terrorism, with the assassination of the Tsar as its main aim. Ishutin laid down that a member of *Hell* must change his name and remain unmarried, having no family ties or friends, and he also put it about that *Hell* was only part of a large-scale European Revolutionary Committee, thus pioneering the technique of mystification later developed by Nechayev.

Some of these details take one into a world of adolescent fantasy, not to say abnormal psychology. But the group was brought down to earth with a jolt when a member, Dmitry Karakozov, suddenly announced that he intended to go ahead and kill the Tsar. It was one thing to discuss tsaricide in the abstract, and quite another to find someone waving the revolver with which he meant to do the job. The others tried to stop Karakozov, but he had made up his mind.

Karakozov was a typical Nihilist to look at, with the usual pale face, long hair and untidy clothes. He also had the usual interrupted university career, but added to such conventional features of the Nihilist certain eccentricities which seem to take one into the lunatic fringe of the movement. They included repeated threats to commit suicide, for which purpose he bought poison. Just before announcing his intention to kill the Tsar, he left a message saying that he was going to drown himself, instead of which he appears to have made a pilgrimage to the famous Monastery of the Trinity and St Sergius near Moscow. A more dangerous aberration was observed when he distributed a manifesto announcing in advance his intention to kill the Tsar, whom he described as the chief enemy of the people. A copy of this document was sent to the authorities by an anonymous informer, but these were carefree days when neither Nihilists nor police bothered much about security precautions, and no action was taken.

The attempt took place on 4 April 1866, as the Emperor was returning from a walk in the Summer Garden in St Petersburg. He was about to get into his carriage when Karakozov suddenly fired his revolver, only to miss – his arm jogged at the last moment, according to officially fostered rumour, by a loyal artisan. But the assassin was an excited young man whose trigger finger may not have been very steady in any case.

The results of the episode were unfortunate for all concerned, even for the humble loyalist who reputedly saved the Tsar's life, only to die of drink after being granted the official rank of honorary gentleman and indulging in a strenuous orgy of celebration. Karakozov himself was tried and duly hanged in public before a large crowd on the Smolensk Field in St Petersburg. Ishutin was also condemned to death and brought to the scaffold, but at the last moment his sentence was commuted to one of penal servitude for life. *Hell* and *The Organization* now came to an end, many of their members being tried with Karakozov and Ishutin, and sent to penal servitude in Siberia.

Where holders of supreme power are concerned, it may be said that nothing concentrates the mind so wonderfully as being shot at, and the Emperor now resolved to quell Nihilism by taking harsher counter-measures. Count Michael Muravyov, called 'Hanger Muravyov' because of his treatment of Polish rebels a few years earlier, was put in charge of the investigation into the Karakozov conspiracy. Police repression was intensified; the two leading radical journals, *The Contemporary* and *Russian Word*, were permanently banned; and liberal reforms already enacted were watered down by various supplementary provisions. Count Dmitry Tolstoy, a notorious reactionary, was made Minister of Education, pledged to a policy of stifling revolutionary sentiment in the high schools and universities, which were its main breeding ground. To this movement of repression, sparked off by Karakozov's revolver shot, the name White Terror was given.

After Karakozov's attempt, all was fairly quiet for two or three years, but then the spectacular figure of Sergey Nechayev, a great promoter of his peculiar brand of secret society, suddenly burst on the arena. Nechayev claimed that 'Karakozov was merely the prologue. Now, friends, let us start the drama.'[13]

Deriving as it does from Latin *nihil*, the name Nihilist seems to imply a belief either in nothing at all or in destruction for its own sake. In fact, as has been seen, Nihilists were not men of little or no faith. Far from it: they mostly believed passionately in something, if only in a hotch-potch involving revolution, the Russian peasant, Chernyshevsky, some kind of Socialism, the idea of progress, science, materialism and so on. They preached destruction often enough, but chiefly as a means to an end, the necessary prelude to some dimly conceived, but fervently desired new order. Still, one often seems to discern a powerful death-wish beating behind the high-minded sentiments with which they rationalized such urges.

In Nechayev's case this death-wish (death for others rather than himself) was openly preached and effectively practised. No one went further in urging destruction for its own sake without any nonsense about creating a better world. Nechayev explicitly claimed to have 'an entirely negative plan . . . total annihilation'.[14] This formula, repeated *ad nauseam* with minor variations, more or less makes up his message to the world.

Nechayev became a ruthless murderer, blackmailer, extortioner and confidence trickster. His special talent was the concoction of imaginary secret societies, which he peddled to the credulous as others have sold shares in non-existent gold mines. He had a knack of dominating such varied associates as the famous *émigré* anarchist Bakunin, who was thirty years his senior, and the politically unsophisticated warders and guards of the Peter and Paul Fortress, from which he conducted an elaborate correspondence with the assassins of Alexander II in 1881.

Nechayev began operations as an external student of St Petersburg University in 1868. Summoned for questioning by the police over some minor matter, he decided to flee abroad, having first spread a false trail suggesting that he had been arrested and taken to an unknown Russian gaol. He then appeared in Geneva and boasted to Bakunin that he had just escaped from the Peter and Paul Fortress.

Bakunin had a lively imagination of his own. When Nechayev announced himself as delegate of a 'Russian Revolutionary Committee', Bakunin capped this tall story by appointing the young man member of the equally imaginary 'Russian Section of the World Revolutionary Alliance'. He gave him the number 2771, thus cunningly suggesting that there were other members too.[15] Despite such flashes of superior technique, it was Nechayev who held the upper hand over Bakunin. They published revolutionary pamphlets together, including the notorious *Catechism of a Revolutionary*. Here the theme of total, merciless destruction occurs as a repeated refrain. 'Day and night he [the revolutionary] must have only one thought, one aim: pitiless destruction. He pursues his aim coldly and relentlessly, and must be prepared to perish himself, as also to destroy with his own hands anyone who stands in his way.' This comes from Article Six of the *Catechism*, but it might equally well come from any of the twenty-five other articles of that turgid piece of rhetoric.

Before long Nechayev did indeed succeed in destroying others with his own hands, and also in accomplishing his own downfall. Returning to Russia in August 1869, he set up the organization called *People's Vengeance*, composed of cells each having five members. Since none of the cells was in touch with any of the others, the conspirators had only Nechayev's word for it that there were any other cells at all, or indeed that the Secret Revolutionary Committee, to which he constantly referred, was more than a figment of his imagination. The Committee's orders, which Nechayev would pass on for immediate unquestioning execution, had a curious way of coinciding with his own apparent inclinations. But he did occasionally allow his followers glimpses of the wider picture, as when he told them that world revolution would break out on 19 February 1870.

Before that fateful date arrived Nechayev took the opportunity to commit the first Nihilist murder of importance. A student member of his organization, improbably named Ivan Ivanovich Ivanov, began to query the very existence of the mysterious Committee whose agent Nechayev claimed to be. This insubordination put the leader's prestige at hazard, while also giving him the chance to strengthen revolutionary discipline by implicating other cell-members in a joint crime: the collective murder of Ivanov.

On the evening of 21 November 1869 the victim was accordingly lured to the premises of the Moscow School of Agriculture, a hotbed of revolutionary sentiment, where Nechayev did him to death by shooting and strangulation, assisted without great enthusiasm by three dupes. Technically speaking, the job was not a great success. The minor conspirators panicked and Nechayev was badly bitten on the hand in the course of the victim's death agony. The body, dumped in a half-frozen pond, was discovered four days later and the whole squalid affair was immortalized, though not depicted with strict accuracy, in Dostoyevsky's *Devils*, where Shatov plays Ivanov to Peter Verkhovensky's Nechayev.

Nechayev's accomplices were arrested and tried. Meanwhile he had slipped quietly back to Switzerland, whence he was extradited in 1872 as a common murderer not entitled to political asylum. At his trial he bore himself with insolent defiance ('I refuse to be the slave of your tyrannical government'), as also at the ceremony of his civil execution, when he bellowed above the customary drum-roll: 'There will soon be a guillotine here to chop off the heads of those who brought me to this place! Down with the Tsar!'

Dismayed by reports of these proceedings, Alexander II countermanded the sentence brought in by the court, of twenty years' penal servitude to be followed by permanent exile to Siberia, and gave orders for Nechayev to be held for life in the Peter and Paul Fortress. It was now that he began patiently recruiting his gaolers, as revolutionary couriers, so that he was able after eight years' silence to exchange letters with the *People's Will* party in early 1881, at the very time when final plans for Alexander II's assassination were being made. Nechayev conducted a sort of correspondence course in tsaricide for the benefit of *People's Will*, trying to embellish their assassination plans with enterprising flourishes of his own, which proved impractical.

The conspirators had been astonished to learn that this demoniac figure was still alive, and would have been glad to organize his escape as well as the Tsar's assassination, had their resources stretched to both projects. The episode shows how much prestige Nechayev still enjoyed among Nihilists as a legendary figure with a heroic past, though they often objected to him as too ruthless; in the end even Bakunin found Nechayev too rich a mixture for his taste.

After the Tsar's death the disclosure of Nechayev's contacts with *People's Will* led to a purge of the guards of the Peter and Paul Fortress, and Nechayev himself was thrust deeper into the dungeons beyond the ken of the outside world. He died a few years later, from causes variously reported as scurvy, tuberculosis and being hanged in his cell. It had been an existence full of sound, fury and pointless cruelty, but it is significant that the eventual assassins of the Tsar were prepared to accept this sanguinary monster and most Nihilist of Nihilists as their blood-brother.

5

Loving the Peasants

The threshold of the 1870s has now been crossed, and the question arises whether it is proper to continue applying the term Nihilist to those who, in the new decade, upheld the traditions of the old.

The seasoned terrorist Sergey Kravchinsky, writing under the pseudonym Stepnyak, regarded Nihilism as ending with the 1860s, drawing as he did a clear distinction between that decade (as the age of Nihilists) and the 1870s: the age of revolutionaries. In his *Underground Russia* he comes near to suggesting that every Russian Nihilist was suddenly transformed, like Cinderella in reverse, into the prince-like figure of a revolutionary as the clock struck twelve on New Year's eve 1870. It was a total transformation, according to Kravchinsky, not just a change of name, because Nihilists were selfish and concerned only with their own happiness, while revolutionaries sought happiness only for others and sacrificed their own. Their ideal was a life of suffering and a martyr's death. 'By some strange quirk of fate [Kravchinsky continues] the first of these types [the Nihilist], who was not and could not be known anywhere outside his own country, has not been given a name in [Western] Europe, whereas the second, who won such terrifying notoriety, received the name of his predecessor. What irony!'[16]

Things were not, in fact, quite so clear-cut. Russian revolutionaries did not suddenly manifest themselves in 1871, nor was self-sacrifice a monopoly of the later decade. As has been noted, the 1860s did not lack revolutionary martyrs, among whom Rakhmetov's creator and imitators were numbered. Nor did the word Nihilist drop out of use in Russia in 1871. Dostoyevsky, for example, regularly employs it in his *Diary of a Writer* (1873–81), though to

An unsuccessful assassination. The Nihilist attempt on the life of General Baron Drenteln, head of security police, in March 1879

The Nihilist Mlodetsky being taken to execution after his unsuccessful attempt at assassinating Loris-Melikov

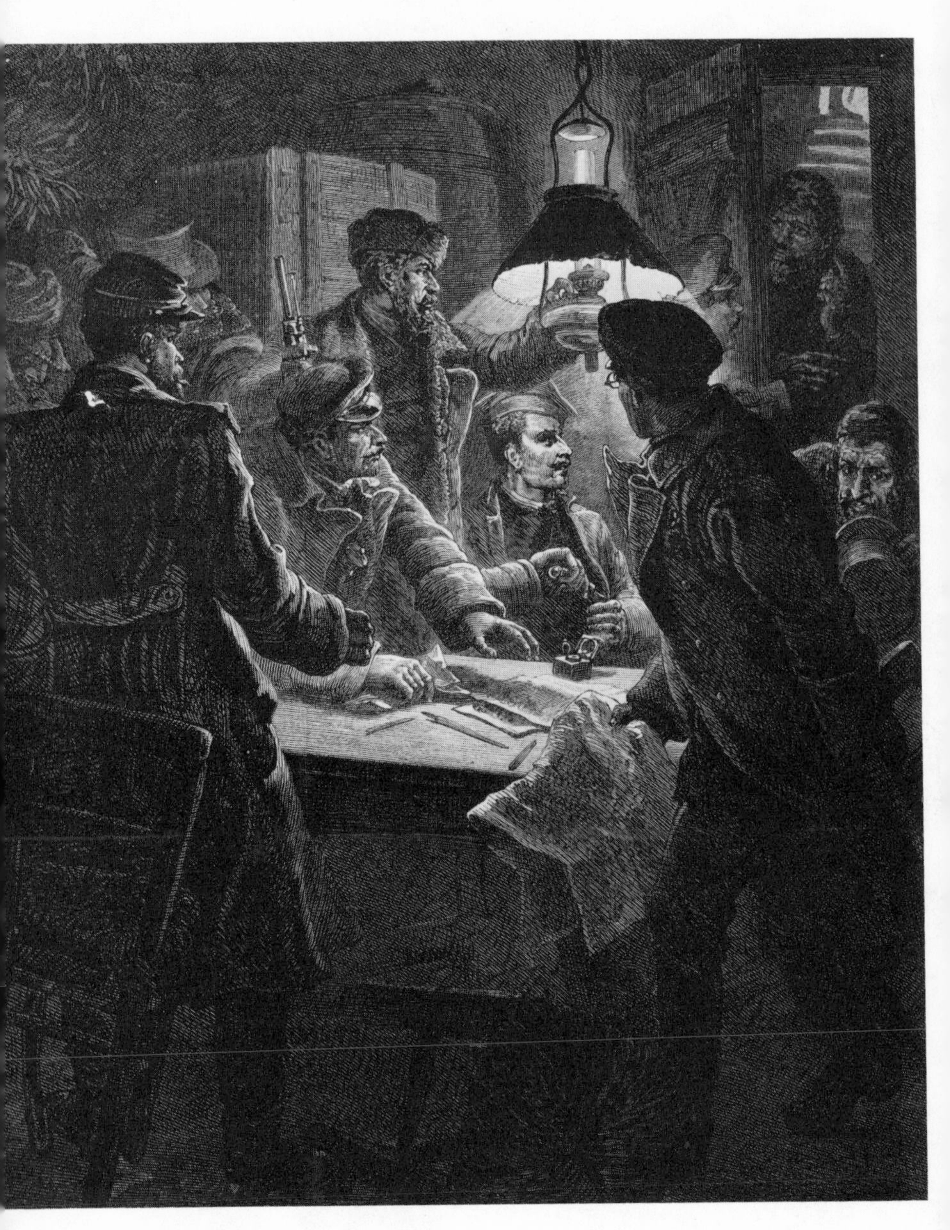

A Nihilist meeting surprised

A police raid on a Nihilist printing press in St Petersburg

The arrest of a suspected Nihilist in St Petersburg

Prisoners leaving St Petersburg for Siberia, November 1879

The arrest of a propagandist

Three leading contributors to *The Contemporary:* Chernyshevsky, Dobrolyubov and Mikhaylov

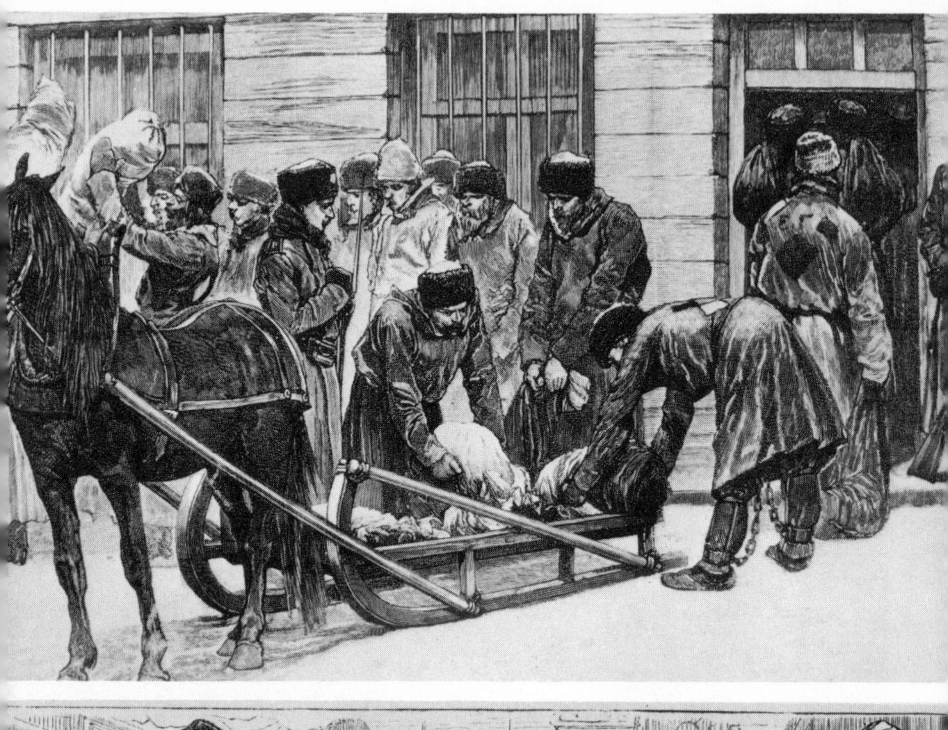

A painting dated 1882 of a Nihilist refusing confession (State Tretyakov Gallery)

above opposite Prisoners unloading sledges at Krasnoyarsk in Siberia

below opposite Political prisoners at a railway station

Woman selling food to prisoners at Krasnoyarsk prison in Siberia

above opposite The Peter and Paul Fortress, St Petersburg

below opposite Schlüsselburg Fortress at the point where the River Neva leaves Lake Ladoga

A Siberian town in 1870 – a typical place of exile for political prisoners

describe persons holding political views on the left of his own – which meant almost everybody. Kravchinsky himself does not always follow his own precept either, the terms Nihilist and revolutionary being sometimes confused and used interchangeably in his own memoirs. Other revolutionaries of the 1870s are also found referring to themselves as Nihilists, though often ironically because of the pejorative tone which the word had acquired.

On the whole those described as Nihilists or revolutionaries were exactly the same people, except that the first term expressed antipathy and the second approval. It is therefore natural that, as in the 1860s, some supporters of violent political upheaval explicitly dissociated themselves from Nihilism in the following decade. To Vera Figner, for example, Nihilism was a matter of dress and behaviour, not of political conviction and tactics. Before going over entirely to the terrorist movement at the end of the 1870s, she and one of her sisters had been involved, like many of their colleagues, in revolutionary welfare-work in the Russian countryside. 'Luckily for us [she wrote of this period in her memoirs] our manners and appearance made it impossible for people to call us Nihilists.'[17] To the Figner girls it would have seemed bad form to parade in Nihilist rig, quite apart from the foolishness of attracting police attention by doing so. But though Figner would not have it that she and her sister were Nihilists, the word was still fully alive to her as applied to the late 1870s, and was by no means tied to a bygone age.

Kravchinsky clearly exaggerated, but it is true that the new decade brought a noticeable change of style and tempo into the political underground, whether it be called revolutionary or Nihilist. At the beginning of the 1870s a reaction took place against the excesses of Nechayev, and the emphasis switched for a time from conspiratorial terrorism to peaceful propaganda. At the same time the movement broadened its base, with the result that those concerned soon came to be numbered by the hundred or thousand rather than by the dozen or score, while still forming only a tiny fraction of the total population. This was how things stood in the early 1870s, but the story of the decade is one of increasing violence, culminating in the assassination of the Tsar.

The first important conspiratorial movement of the decade was that of the Chaykovskyites. They took their name from Nicholas Chaykovsky, who assumed the leading role when the original founder, Mark Natanson, was arrested in 1871. The group was based on St Petersburg and operated between 1870 and 1873, numbering some thirty active members in the capital, and having branches in Moscow and elsewhere.

By Nihilist standards it was a gentle affair. The Chaykovskyites' aim was to spread Socialism by the use of officially permitted printed material, though they also came to employ illegal matter, and acquired their own clandestine press. They were the first underground political group to make a serious attempt to influence the industrial workers of the capital, but the movement also acknowledged a debt to the 'people' at large, which in effect meant to the peasants. This makes it the first important Russian Populist movement.

The Russian peasantry was now becoming more and more the focus of anguished revolutionary hopes. The peasants formed by far the most numerous social class, to which over four fifths of the population belonged. In other words they were about eighty times as numerous as industrial workers, though it should be noted that for various reasons the distinction between peasant and worker in Russia was not hard and fast.

The cultural and psychological gap between intellectual and peasant was enormous. Most peasants were illiterate; even by the end of the century less than a quarter of the rural population aged between nine and forty-nine could read and write. Peasants wore peasant clothes and spoke in peasant speech. They were instinctively loyal to the Tsar and to the ritual of the Orthodox Church; it was the landlords and officials whom they considered their enemies, and against whom they put on an armour of pretended stupidity which often concealed considerable shrewdness. Many lived in abject poverty, being not much better off than their own livestock, so that it was easy for the educated Russian to think of them as semi-domesticated beasts. Thus, however sincerely Russian intellectuals might set themselves to repay a debt to the peasantry, they tended to remain peasant-lovers in the sense in which some people are animal-lovers.

Nihilists found it difficult to understand why the peasant masses showed so little interest in organized violent upheaval. It was infuriating to see so many people so badly treated, who yet refused to turn against society other than sporadically and half-heartedly.

They would not respond to a call for revolutionary action. Yet it seemed necessary to act fast because of the interpretation commonly put on a special Russian institution much discussed by social thinkers: the village commune. These self-governing bodies (which managed some village affairs, including land distribution, by decisions taken collectively) were claimed as unique to the Slav world, and seemed to open the prospect of a special Russian form of social revolution not available to other countries. Somehow it was easy to see a transition from autocratic to Socialist Russia, provided that the commune was made the basis. Meanwhile industrialization was proceeding apace, and Russian capitalism, complete with *bourgeoisie* and proletariat, was all too swiftly coming into being. If this process were allowed to go on too long, the commune (it was felt) might be thrust into the background, together with the special Russian short cut to Socialism which it seemed to make possible. Hence the importance of promoting rural revolution before it was too late.

Such were the preoccupations of a period which witnessed the strange phenomenon called 'the pilgrimages to the people'. Young men and women, usually on their own or in groups of two or three, spent the summers of 1873 and 1874 (the latter was called the 'mad summer') among the peasants, sleeping in peasant huts or barns, wearing peasant dress, doing manual work and trying to enlighten or agitate the rural population. They usually plied a trade, such as cobbling, dyeing or carpentry; somehow one does not often hear of them helping with the harvest, no doubt too hard a job for anyone but a peasant born and bred. So far as young intellectuals were concerned, this was almost a mass movement; only a few hundred or at the most a thousand or two took part, but then the over-all number of young Russian intellectuals was not very great. The pilgrimages were not centrally planned, but came about spontaneously, as many contemporary observers have pointed out.

The better to merge with the landscape, some young people decked themselves out in rural garb, for all the world as if they were off to a fancy-dress ball. They were liable to overdo things, imagining that the more primitive their apparel, the more gratefully the peasantry would clasp them to its homespun bosom. But this did not quite work out. The peasants tended to be suspicious of a shabby stranger, even though they might be worse dressed themselves.

During one well-documented pilgrimage to the people, Vladimir Debogory-Mokriyevich and a companion, both heavily disguised as villagers, eventually did make friends with an elderly Ukrainian peasant, but the old man later confided that he had been appalled when the two Nihilists first descended on his hut. 'Proper frightened I was when I first see you at the gate . . . "What do they want with me?" thinks I. "Them and those nasty beards! Hope to God I never run across the likes of them in the middle of the woods!" '[18] (The episode took place in a part of the Ukraine where the peasants went clean-shaven.) Since the peasants also mistrusted people in 'German dress', their name for the normal clothing of educated Russians, the problem of what to wear on pilgrimage seemed well-nigh insoluble.

Some Nihilists went further and tried to impress the peasants by pretending to be illiterate: another mistake. A peasant might be unable to read and write himself, but literacy was a skill which he held in great respect.

Two main strains developed in the movement to the people, each being associated with the teaching of a leading Russian *émigré* political thinker.

The milder strain was that of the Lavrovists, who put their faith mainly in propaganda, basing themselves on the teaching of Peter Lavrov, who had emigrated to Paris in 1870, and began publishing the journal *Forward!* (which became the chief organ of Russian Populism) in Switzerland in 1873. Lavrov eventually changed his views and came to support terrorism, but in the 1870s 'Lavrovist' was regularly used to describe those who thought that revolution must come after a long process of preparation by propaganda; for which reason they were also called 'propagandists'.

The Lavrovists gradually lost ground to the more violent school of thought associated with Michael Bakunin, the Russian revolutionary anarchist who was also active in Switzerland, and had once been a fellow-conspirator of Nechayev. Bakuninists believed in pushing the peasants into immediate revolution, not in preparing them for it by a long process of training. The peasants were ready for revolt, it was argued, and even if they were not it would do them no harm to be pushed in at the deep end. 'Whoever loves the people leads them into cannon fire,' was a saying of the period, but unfortunately it was often the people who were shot at, not those who led them under fire. This more militant attitude earned the Bakuninists the nickname of 'rioters' (*buntari*).

Whether Lavrovist or Bakuninist in emphasis, the pilgrimages of 1873 and 1874 were acknowledged failures. Quite unable to imagine what the touring Nihilists were about, the villagers themselves often handed them over to the police before they had time to explain. Nor was the Russian countryside an ideal place in which to organize conspiracy. The Nihilist, who might have gone undetected on St Petersburg's Nevsky Prospekt, attracted attention as a stranger the moment he set foot in a Russian village, however lovingly he might have disguised himself as a yokel.

Besides, the policy of provoking peasant riots was based on a misunderstanding. Though minor local disturbances were going on independently of revolutionary intellectuals somewhere in the Russian countryside during most of the period, the peasants could not be supplied with arms on a suitable scale, quite apart from the fact that they were simply not ripe for organized revolution. Befuddled by historical precedents – those of the Russian and Ukrainian peasant and Cossack revolts under Stenka Razin, the Haydamaks and Pugachov in the seventeenth and eighteenth centuries – the Nihilists toured the Razin, Haydamak and Pugachov territory on the Volga, and in the south and east of European Russia generally, hoping to find embers still smouldering which they could fan into a blaze. Noting also that the French Revolution had been preceded by isolated peasant revolts, they calculated that by re-enacting the same prologue on Russian soil they would automatically bring on the main drama. But in all this they showed themselves the slaves of half-baked ideas and false historical parallels.

The greatest success in hatching rural conspiracy by Bakuninist tactics was achieved in the Chigirin area on the River Dnieper near Kiev. Revolts had already broken out there, without Nihilist participation, in the early 1870s, because the poorer peasants were dissatisfied with the land allotted to them. These disturbances were brutally quelled in 1875, the peasants who would not submit being flogged and having troops quartered in their villages for a time. The situation looked ripe for exploitation, and three revolutionaries – Stefanovich, Deutsch and Bokhanovsky – decided to move in. They printed copies of a spurious charter purporting to come from the

Tsar, and urged the peasants to prepare a secret militia for a revolt against the common enemies of both Tsar and peasant: landlords and officials.

By autumn 1877 the conspirators had about a thousand peasants under arms, but the arms themselves were discouragingly primitive, usually home-made pikes. There was systematic oath-taking and much emphasis on secrecy, but the truth was bound to leak out in the end. When it did, hundreds of peasants were arrested and many exiled to Siberia. The three Nihilists were also clapped in Kiev gaol, from which, as later to be described, they were rescued by a daring ruse.

No one bothered to rescue the peasants. Nihilists were always talking about the wrongs done to the common man, but were all too inclined to compound those wrongs themselves by treating the peasantry as political cannon-fodder. Vera Figner, for example, ingeniously explains the revolutionary advantages of playing on the widespread peasant illusion that all would be well if only direct contact could be established with the Tsar by sending village delegates to petition him personally.

'The fate of such suppliants [she points out] is well known. Some are exiled to distant provinces, some are arrested and others are taken home under police escort. Bitter experience will show the peasants that they have nothing to hope for from the Tsar, but must rely solely on their own efforts to secure a better future.'[19] An accurate calculation, perhaps, but not much consolation to the dupes and their families.

For some time before the Chigirin affair the movement to the people had been leading to widespread arrests, but many of those concerned were not brought to trial for several years. Meanwhile some were freed on bail, while others were held in the St Petersburg Remand Prison, where conditions were harsh, but did not break their spirit, as many showed when brought to trial.

The biggest trial of the period, that of the '193', began in St Petersburg in October 1877. It was an indecorous occasion, with many of the accused hurling abuse at their judges, who from time to time lost control of the proceedings and had to have the court cleared.

The hero of the '193', Ippolit Myshkin, denounced the court in words which were widely repeated and echoed round the Empire.

'This is no trial [he told his judges], but a farce or something worse: something more revolting and shameful than a brothel. There a woman sells her body because she's poor, but here – '. At this point the presiding judge ordered Myshkin's removal. Gendarmes rushed up, and an officer tried to hold his hand over the orator's mouth, but he broke away and continued: 'Here Senators [the judges], out of baseness and slavishness, and for the sake of promotion and high salaries, trade away other people's lives, truth and justice – .' He was hauled away still trying to speak. Intransigent to the end, he was eventually shot in 1885 in Schlüsselburg Fortress for attacking a prison officer.

When the trial ended in January 1878, the sentences imposed on the '193' proved unexpectedly light, nearly half of the accused being acquitted outright. But the day after the end of the trial was also the day chosen for the attempted assassination of General Trepov, to be described shortly. As a result of this the sentences imposed on the '193' were considerably increased and fourteen of the condemned received penal servitude – instead of Myshkin alone, as previously ordained. The affair had been grossly mismanaged by the authorities, who might have done better to be more lenient or more severe. As it was, many a peaceful propagandist among the '193' lived on to fight another day as an embittered terrorist. Among them was Sophia Perovsky, who had been a Chaykovskyite early in the decade, but was now approaching her initiation as a practitioner of terror. Her acquittal was to prove expensive.

6

The Rise of Terrorism

Three main tendencies can be seen in the development of Russian underground political activity in the late 1870s.

In the first place there was a drift of revolutionaries away from the land. After the failure of the pilgrimages to the people, and of attempts to heal, teach or agitate the peasantry, disillusionment set in and activity became more concentrated on the towns. Those who continued to hanker after work among the peasants were now ridiculed by more urban-minded revolutionaries as 'yokels', and in any case such work had become almost impossible.

The second trend was an increasingly embittered hostility to the government, inflamed by the inept treatment of revolutionaries during imprisonment and trial, and also by the development of the Russo-Turkish War of 1877–8. Though the war was won by Russia, it revealed gross incompetence in the conduct of military affairs, and thus further discredited the authorities. Nor was it clear to Russians why they should go to war to give Bulgaria privileges which they themselves were still denied: it was noted that the Bulgarians, after being freed from the Turks, were granted a constitution such as their liberators had long hoped for in vain.

The third tendency among revolutionaries of the late 1870s was an increased hankering after a central organization to control and co-ordinate their activities. This led to the foundation of a second group called *Land and Freedom*, which revived the name of the earlier secret society. The new title was not officially adopted until 1878, but much the same body of people had been in association for some two years before that under the names, first of *Troglodytes*, and then of the *Revolutionary-Populist Group of the North*. They had also come, more loosely, to refer to themselves as Populists. This society or party did not last long, being dissolved in 1879, but during 1876–9 it was the most influential group among Russian revolutionaries, exercising general supervision over the developing terrorist movement. Though not a tightly controlled and disciplined revolutionary nucleus, it marked a step in that direction. It belonged to the Bakuninist rather than the Lavrovist school of thought, and so its dominance reflects the growing intransigence of the Nihilist-Revolutionary-Populist movement and a victory for the hard line of the so-called rioters over the milder policies of the propagandists.

The period of revolutionary terrorism and assassination from 1878 to 1881 was opened, suitably enough, by a Nihilist girl. It was on 24 January 1878 that Vera Zasulich shot and wounded General Trepov, City Prefect of St Petersburg.

The origins of this affair go back to a political demonstration held in the Square of Our Lady of Kazan on 6 December 1876. Disaffected workers had decided to show students and intellectuals that others too could demonstrate. One feature of this ill-organized occasion was the unfurling of a red banner bearing the slogan 'Land and Freedom', which had not yet been formally adopted as the name of the Party. The police broke up the meeting, making some arrests, and among those seized was a Nihilist commonly known as Bogolyubov. Far from being a ringleader, he had not even taken part in the demonstration, but had only come along as it was dispersing, and so his trial and sentence to fifteen years' penal servitude were a cruel injustice. The authorities, it appears, wanted a scapegoat; and here was an intellectual with a revolutionary record who seemed a suitable candidate.

Bogolyubov's troubles had only just begun. The next act of the drama took place in the Remand Prison in St Petersburg while he was still there after sentence. The prison happened to be full of Nihilists awaiting trial in another case, that of '193'. Many had been in custody for three or four years and there was a tense, mutinous atmosphere.

The prison authorities began to complain of growing indiscipline among the inmates, and one day in July 1877 General Trepov arrived to look into the matter. It was not a good moment to defy an inspecting notability by refusing to take your cap off, but this is what the unlucky Bogolyubov did. Trepov lost his temper and tore the cap from his head, or (according to one version) attacked him with his fists, and then shouted that he was to be flogged. The punishment was duly meted out on the following day in a corridor of the gaol before some of the other prisoners, and so severely that it was said to have caused further misfortunes: the victim became insane in Kharkov Prison in 1880.

The immediate effect of the flogging was to start a prison mutiny. Bars of cell windows were torn off and beaten against the doors, and prisoners were reputedly tied up by warders, beaten, kicked and hauled unconscious to the punishment cells. Outside the prison Trepov's act created widespread indignation by no means confined to professed revolutionaries. A Russian gentleman's honour was especially sensitive where the striking of blows was involved, and so Bogolyubov's punishment was taken as a monstrous affront to the whole revolutionary movement, staffed as it very largely was by young people who retained certain social pretensions. As for that common event, the flogging of obstreperous peasants, it is true that the Nihilists deplored it; but they looked on it rather from above, considering themselves, as it were, representatives of a society for the prevention of cruelty to members of an inferior species.

Vera Zasulich simply wanted to avenge an intolerable insult, and was not personally acquainted with either Bogolyubov or Trepov. Nor was she the only Nihilist to vow revenge on the tyrant: merely the one who, to the annoyance of several others, got her blow in first. She began by seeking audience with the General as one of a crowd of sundry petitioners such as regularly thronged the reception-rooms of high-ranking Russian officials. At the crucial moment she removed a revolver from her muff and fired; Trepov fell wounded, after which she calmly allowed herself to be arrested. The victim eventually recovered, saying how pleased he was to have stopped a bullet which might otherwise have been directed at the sacred person of the Emperor himself.

The final act in the drama took place at Zasulich's trial. Her guilt was so evident that the authorities risked the liberal gesture of allowing trial by jury. It seemed safe enough: the young woman herself admitted firing the shot, there were witnesses, and the lethal weapon was available in evidence, so what else could any jury do but find her guilty? After that the presiding judge might be relied upon for a stiff sentence.

The rigging of public trials was later developed into a special

Russian art form, but in 1878 it was still in its infancy, as was the very institution of open courts. All the calculations misfired. The presiding judge, it turned out, was not easily bullied, and as for the jury, they blandly found the girl not guilty in spite of all the evidence. The verdict was popular, being applauded in court even by conservative officials and their wives who found the spectacle a pleasant change from visiting the opera.

A minor riot developed in the street outside as the heroine emerged from court. It was feared that she might be seized by gendarmes in spite of the acquittal, as arrests could be carried out and exile imposed administratively (without recourse to the courts). But friends spirited her away; they were assisted by an excited young man who shot himself, or was shot by a gendarme, in the middle of the general confusion, so creating a diversion.

The episode was calculated to inflame Nihilist militancy. With the flogging of Bogolyubov, the authorities offered a provocative insult. Then they went on to dither in manipulating the creaky machinery of despotism, and seemed to have lost their nerve entirely. To be vicious and vulnerable at the same time is to ask for trouble, and the Nihilists now determined to close in for the kill. The result was the three years of revolutionary terror which ended with the Tsar's assassination. It was Vera Zasulich who launched the campaign: a doubtful honour, though Trepov himself hardly cries out for sympathy and Nihilists were by no means the only people who thought that he thoroughly deserved what he got.

The series of Nihilist killings following the Trepov affair are sometimes referred to as a wave of terror. But the number of successful operations of this kind carried out between January 1878 and the death of the Tsar is surprisingly small. There were only three real assassinations, though others too were killed, including several police informers and *agents provocateurs* in the ranks of the Nihilists themselves together with some policemen, passers-by and others. The tally would have been larger if the Nihilists had been able to shoot straight; General Trepov and the Tsar were not the only walking monuments to their poor marksmanship.

By comparison with mid-twentieth-century political terror – by the standards, say, of Cyprus, Kenya and Vietnam – this was a tame affair, as also by comparison with terrorism and counter-terrorism in imperial Russia itself in the first decade of the twentieth century.

But more value was placed on human life in the age of Nihilism, and the people involved did not take these events lightly. Far from it: Nihilist assassinations and other terrorist acts threw Tsar and government into a flurry of anxiety and activity. They made serious, determined and by no means stupid attempts to deal with the problem, trying by turns to pacify and intimidate the revolutionaries, who numbered but a few hundreds and were only a tiny proportion of the population at large. The key to the problem was never found, however. It was one of the authorities' aims to enlist non-extremist elements in society against the Nihilists, but this they somehow could not manage, and educated Russians in general adopted the role of spectators at a gladiatorial contest, rather than of persons whose own interests were involved in one way or another. As for the 'dark people' (the peasants), few of them had much inkling of what was going on.

The first arena of violence was in southern Russia – what is now called the Ukraine – and especially in Kiev and Odessa. On 30 January 1878 the Odessa police raided the lodgings of the revolutionary Ivan Kovalsky, who kept a secret printing press. He defended himself desperately with revolver and dagger, while friends burnt documents and shouted appeals to the crowd in the street from the balcony of the premises. Kovalsky thus founded a tradition of shooting it out with the police, which became common practice during the next few years. After trial before a military tribunal, accompanied by riots outside the courtroom, he was sentenced to death and was shot on 2 August. Apart from persons involved in attempts on the life of the Tsar, Kovalsky's was the first Russian political execution in memory; but it was soon followed by others.

The rest of Alexander II's reign saw the execution by hanging of twenty-one Nihilists in all, in addition to which five more were hanged in April 1881 for complicity in the events of 1 March. Thus the authorities killed more Nihilists than *vice versa*, though, as already indicated, this was on both sides a ripple of terror rather than a tidal wave.

There was further violence in southern Russia when a police spy was killed by revolutionaries on the night of 1–2 February at Rostov-on-Don; a notice of execution posted in Kiev bore the seal of the Executive Committee of the Russian Socialist Revolutionary

Party. This mysterious Executive Committee had a shadowy existence, being a piece of spoof in the style of Nechayev devised by the pioneer of southern terrorism, Valerian Osinsky. On the evening of 23 February, Osinsky shot the public prosecutor of Kiev, leaving him for dead after firing once or twice. But the victim was unhurt: saved, according to one theory, by a thick fur coat which warded off the bullets.

The southern Nihilists struck again to more effect when Gregory Popko stabbed to death Captain Geyking of the Kiev gendarmerie on a corner of the main thoroughfare of the city on 25 May. Popko escaped after fatally shooting a doorkeeper who tried to stop him and wounding a policeman. Geyking was an unhappy choice of victim, at least according to the lapsed Nihilist Leo Tikhomirov, who suggests in his memoirs that this officer of gendarmes was only concerned to 'go through the motions' of his job, and that he treated revolutionaries kindly. Geyking was so popular with them, according to Tikhomirov, that he did not feel the need to take safety precautions, for which reason this was a cowardly murder done to gain cheap publicity.[20] Others took a different view of Geyking. But leaving his personal qualities on one side, it does seem to be a general tendency of assassination, whether in Russia or elsewhere, that comparatively harmless persons suffer while more appropriate victims escape.

Two days after killing Geyking the Kiev terrorists pulled off a bloodless *coup* in the Scarlet Pimpernel tradition. Three Nihilists – Stefanovich, Deutsch and Bokhanovsky, who may be remembered for their part in preparing a peasant revolt in the Chigirin district – were held pending trial in the city gaol, famed as an impregnable fortress. Michael Frolenko, an especially enterprising southern conspirator, managed to obtain employment on the prison staff, and rose within a few months to the position of chief warder; the previous incumbent, a heavy drinker, was lured into resigning his post by the promise of a (non-existent) job as foreman in a distillery. On the night of 27 May the three men, disguised as soldiers or workmen, were simply conducted out of the premises by Frolenko, who had the keys. On the way out one of them accidentally sounded the prison alarm bell in his excitement, but their luck held. Frolenko melted away and the other three spent a week on the Dnieper rowing to a rendezvous downstream and hiding in the reeds whenever they saw another boat.

This was a notable Nihilist operation in which no one was hurt, except for the chief warder, who lost his job. Frolenko went on to help plot the Emperor's assassination. Like a surprising number of other Nihilists he survived the hazards of the era, living on into more dangerous times and attaining an advanced age as a citizen of the Soviet Union.

By mid-1878 the Nihilists of northern Russia were lagging behind those of the south, but on 4 August they asserted their claims with an assassination regarded by connoisseurs as a classic. At nine o'clock in the morning on one of the main streets of St Petersburg, Sergey Kravchinsky walked towards General Mezentsov, Chief of Gendarmes and Head of the Third Section, who was on the way to his office. Kravchinsky held a dagger lightly wrapped in newspaper; after passing the General, he thrust it in his back and twisted it, then leapt into a carriage drawn by Barbarian, a famous trotter, and escaped.

Once again Tikhomirov disparages a noted Nihilist exploit. In his memoirs he describes Kravchinsky as a megalomaniac publicity-seeker who had had to be persuaded to abandon his original plan of cutting the General's head right off with one swish of a heavy sabre specially constructed for the purpose; Kravchinsky was thought to be physically strong enough for this feat of bravado. Tikhomirov also calls Mezentsov's murder a tactical disaster on the grounds that his tenure of office actually favoured revolution, since he was a grossly incompetent police chief and more of a *bon viveur* than a flail of Nihilism.[21] It is true that the police and Third Section had to be thoroughly overhauled soon afterwards; an inquiry revealed that the only efficiently functioning department was that devoted to spying on the private lives of members of the imperial family. So there may be something in what Tikhomirov says. But the attack on Mezentsov was not planned in a spirit of frivolity; he was held responsible for the more severe sentences imposed after trial on some of the defendants in the Case of the '193'. As a piece of publicity the assassination of the Chief of Gendarmes seemed like a triumph of timing, because it came two days after Kovalsky's execution in Odessa, and so looked like a clever piece of Nihilist counter-punching.

The government's next blow followed a few days later with an edict providing that offences against the State and its employees should from now on be tried by military courts with power to impose the death penalty. This had some effect, since there seem to have been no assassination attempts between that on Mezentsov on 4 August 1878 and the shooting of Governor General Dmitry Kropotkin in Kharkov on the following 9 February, which opened the next terrorist year.

Kropotkin, a cousin of the well-known anarchist Peter Kropotkin, was shot dead in his carriage by a young Jewish revolutionary, Gregory Goldenberg, who escaped for the time being, but was arrested in November of the same year. This proved a disaster for the Nihilists because Goldenberg naïvely confided most of what he knew about his associates to a sympathetic 'revolutionary' who had been put in the same cell, but had in fact turned police informer. The rest was painlessly extracted by a Captain of Gendarmes who induced the bewildered Goldenberg to see himself as the instrument of reconciliation between government and Nihilists. When he realized that he had betrayed his comrades, Goldenberg hanged himself in his cell.

But this is to run ahead. Minor terrorism in early 1879 involved the killing of another police spy, and a gun battle between police and revolutionaries in Kiev on the night of 11 February. But the great event of the season was the attempted shooting of the Tsar himself by Alexander Solovyov: the first time since 1866 that a Russian revolutionary had tried to assassinate Alexander II.

When the Tsar came out for his morning walk in the grounds of the Winter Palace on 2 April, Solovyov was ready for him. He fired five times, only to show himself one more Nihilist badly in need of revolver practice. His Imperial Majesty dodged, 'proceeding [according to an official report of the incident] in a zig-zag manner, moving now to the right, now to the left.'[22] He escaped with a hole in his greatcoat.

The authorities responded by having Solovyov tried by court martial and hanged on 28 May in front of a large crowd including several newspaper correspondents, and also by increasing the number of areas of the country subject to rule by Governor Generals with special powers of control. Kiev, Moscow and Warsaw already had them, and they were now extended by a decree of 5 April to St Petersburg, Kharkov and Odessa, to each of which was assigned a military General who had distinguished himself in the Russo–Turkish War. At the same time the powers of all the Governor Generals were increased. The Nihilists had made all the running in early 1879. Now it was the authorities' turn. They struck back with such effect that sixteen Nihilists were hanged between April and the end of the year, no less than fourteen of whom went to the scaffold in southern Russia. Kiev was the first scene of execution with two triple hangings, but by the middle of August Governor General Totleben of Odessa had been responsible for hanging eight persons within his jurisdiction.

Besides plotting to assassinate, the offences of the sixteen men hanged in 1879 included attempted murder of a police spy; armed resistance to arrest; being in possession of dynamite; and being concerned with the Chigirin Revolt. In one case, that of Dmitry Lizogub, the victim seems to have been guilty of nothing more than spreading revolutionary propaganda and financing the movement. Lizogub's fate aroused strong indignation because he was regarded as a saint of Nihilism. A rich young man and heir to large estates, he spent nothing on himself and rejected the idea of a career or marriage; he was, indeed, much opposed to love, regarding it as a menace to revolutionary activity, and was always upset when one of his friends got married. Though this monkish innocent was hanged, it may be noted that the only three successful assassins of the period (Popko, Kravchinsky and Goldenberg) all escaped the scaffold. Kravchinsky, who went abroad, had a less glorious end to his chequered career, since his further activities included teaching Russian to the English translator Constance Garnett and being run over by a train in London.

Besides those who paid the death penalty, hundreds of Nihilists were also held in prison without trial or sent to exile in Siberia administratively during the same period. It was for his ruthlessness in operating this machinery of oppression that Governor General Totleben obtained his unsavoury reputation. But he escaped assassination. In Kharkov, where there were no executions, Governor General Loris-Melikov pursued a comparatively easy-going policy, but was also detested by the revolutionaries, being regarded as merely a more cunning and 'two-faced' Totleben.

However, Loris-Melikov's methods impressed the Tsar, and he was granted dictatorial powers over the whole country in February 1880. On 20 February the newly-appointed dictator was himself fired at by a revolutionary called Mlodetsky who missed and was hanged with exemplary speed two days later. 1880 continued as another grim year. Though there were fewer assassinations and hangings than in 1879, the campaign to kill the Tsar was going on all the time. But before the assassination campaign is traced, it is worth looking at some of the more everyday details of Nihilist life in the 1870s.

7

The Conspirator - at Large and in Captivity

Nihilists of the 1870s maintained the ascetic tradition of Chernyshevsky's Rakhmetov. Poverty continued to be cultivated, clothes and food were still plain and unadorned, tea remained a principal form of self-indulgence; and though occasional wine and dancing might mark a New Year's Eve or other festival, serious drinking was avoided and vodka frowned upon. From such ascetic practices the flamboyant Sergey Kravchinsky deviated during a period when he used the passport of a Caucasian prince, and could claim that ostentatious plain living was unsuited to his 'cover'. But Kravchinsky was an eccentric, and managed on borrowed money anyway.

For the minority of moneyed Nihilists it was a point of honour to share the general austerity, while contributing as much as possible to the common exchequer. But rich revolutionaries were not numerous, and even they were not always able to tap their own resources. There was thus a chronic shortage of funds with which to finance Nihilist exploits. If money could not be raised in any other way, why not steal from the State, which was itself living on borrowed time, so to speak? In June 1879 a remarkable *coup* was staged in the town of Kherson, where a seventy-foot tunnel was driven into the cellar of the state treasury and the huge sum of over one and a half million roubles seized. But some of the plotters were caught and the money was recovered, apart from ten thousand roubles. Still, this was not a sum to be despised, since the purchasing power of the rouble at the time was, to express it very roughly indeed, that of the pound sterling in England of the middle 1960s.

All Nihilists were secret agents in some degree, and had to equip themselves with the tools of their trade, among which false passports were an important item. It will be remembered that a passport was needed to register with the police on renting an apartment or staying in a hotel, besides which it might be demanded at any time to establish identity. When forging a passport it was safest not just to invent a number, name, date of issue and so on, but rather to duplicate the details of some existing valid passport, in case the police should check with the original place of issue.

When a Nihilist took a false passport, and with it an alias, he became what was called an 'illegal'. Going illegal marked a definite stage in his career, but it was not irrevocable, since he could revert to legality when it seemed safe to do so. And the process could be repeated. Some Nihilists acquired a variety of aliases and conspiratorial nicknames, thus complicating the investigation of their affairs for police and historian alike.

Another Nihilist institution was the conspiratorial apartment. Posing as a married couple and using forged passports, an illegal man and girl would rent a flat at some point of vantage. The ground floor on a corner was ideal, providing facilities for two-way observation of police activities outside, and if necessary a choice of directions in which to make a hurried getaway. It was desirable to use a building where there was enough movement of 'legal' citizens to provide cover for others, and so the Russian urban habit of living in large apartment-blocks had its advantages. Use was also made of country cottages in resorts where the presence of holiday visitors provided camouflage; and where boating, mushrooming and picnicking gave additional cover when necessary.

Once host and hostess were settled in their conspiratorial quarters, other illegals could come and go without the danger and trouble of registering. Some of these apartments simply served as centres for communal living with shared expenses; others were full-scale terrorist headquarters.

Apartment-blocks had porters whom the police expected to act as spies. At one time the Third Section kept a large proportion of the porters of St Petersburg on its pay-roll as potential informers. The results were poor, but porters could often be useful in helping police and gendarmes to take a Nihilist hideout by surprise, and so limit the chance of occupants escaping, destroying incriminating documents and shooting at gendarmes. Rather than knock on the door and ask for it to be opened in the name of the law, raiding gendarmes would induce the porter to announce with a discreet tap that a telegram had arrived.

A raiding party would usually consist of a gendarme officer and a number of ordinary gendarmes together with a district attorney (*prokuror*), whose presence was supposed to safeguard legality. Raids often took place at night, and there were instances of suspects being rudely bundled out of bed, searched with scant courtesy and bullied. But judged by the standards of a more recent age police behaviour was scrupulously correct.

It was the normal practice of the police to keep conspiratorial quarters under surveillance for some time after a raid, with the result that careless visitors found themselves walking straight into a trap. So the occupants would exhibit signals to show friends in the street when the coast was clear. For instance, they might put flowers at a prearranged place on a window-sill, and display or move other objects in a previously agreed way. One simple but effective warning was to break all the windows during a police raid: a danger signal which could not be reversed as quickly or easily as some.

With the rise of revolutionary terrorism, Nihilists took to firing at raiding police, and there were several gun battles with fatalities on both sides. Some Nihilists killed themselves after resisting to the end, and there is an instance showing conspirators prepared to go to even greater lengths: during one of the many tunnelling exploits to be described below, Sophia Perovsky (who acted as landlady of the suburban house in Moscow from which operations were mounted) held herself ready to fire at a large bottle of nitro-glycerine and send raiding gendarmes, plotters and evidence up together in a single holocaust.

It was natural that the police should plant spies among the Nihilists, and that the Nihilists should in turn try to penetrate the police. The honours in this competition go to the Nihilists for their success in placing one of their agents, Nicholas Kletochnikov, in the post of confidential clerk to the investigation department of the Third Section itself. For two years from January 1879, he was able to supply his associates with the names of Third Section agents and of traitors among the Nihilists themselves, together with details of impending raids and even copies of official seals.

Kletochnikov's 'control' was Alexander Mikhaylov, the first

organizer of *People's Will* and the most security-conscious of the Nihilists. He tried to instil the elements of caution into his associates, but was himself caught through a lapse from his own careful standards: trapped in a photographer's shop when he called to collect snapshots of two executed comrades.

Compared with what became customary in later times, the treatment of political prisoners under the Tsars was a model of decorum. It is true that many died in prison of tuberculosis or scurvy brought on by damp, bad air and poor diet, and that many others committed suicide or went mad, which reflects no credit on penal conditions rightly regarded as a scandal of the age. But at least political victims were numbered in hundreds, not millions, and were spared the horrors of the slave camp, of systematic deprivation of food and sleep, and of torture and beatings. 'The prisoner stated that he did not wish to reply' – the frequency with which some such formula occurs in official transcripts of interrogations is itself an eloquent comment on the comparative gentleness of imperial Russian procedures.

With regard to flogging, this was not normally inflicted on political prisoners in imperial times, which is why the Bogolyubov affair provoked such indignation. 'In all the history of our movement [Leo Deutsch states in his memoirs] there had been no single instance of a woman being punished in such a manner; and among the men even, Bogolyubov alone . . . had suffered this indignity.'[23] Deutsch is referring to an occasion in a remote Siberian gaol in 1889 when a woman prisoner was flogged, after which she died, possibly through suicide, and three other women prisoners poisoned themselves in sympathy.

This unhappy episode does not even belong to the period described here, and was entirely exceptional. Political prisoners were ladies and gentlemen, and were treated as such. To guards, warders, gendarmes and interrogators they were 'you' (*vy*): not lumped together with small children, lunatics, animals and peasant convicts as 'thou' (*ty*). They were generally segregated from common criminals and better treated, so that ordinary escaped convicts in Siberia would sometimes try, when recaptured, to pass themselves off as political prisoners, and thus enjoy privileged status if only for a few days until they were detected.

An imprisoned Nihilist might resent the scrupulously correct and ironically solicitous manner of the Colonel of Gendarmes who visited him in his cell, and might reject the offer of an expensive cigar or the opportunity to converse politely in French with the perfumed monster. These things were distasteful to any self-respecting revolutionary. But they were better than being beaten unconscious and crippled for life.

Penal measures applied to political prisoners included exile imposed administratively (without trial) in a designated area of European or Asiatic Russia to which the victim was usually escorted by two gendarmes on a journey of anything from a few hours to several months. It was from such an escort that Sophia Perovsky escaped on the occasion when she 'went illegal'. While being conducted to exile in northern Russia, she was held up at a provincial railway station on the way, where the stationmaster provided a room in which prisoner and escorting gendarmes could spend a few hours. In the middle of the night she was able to steal out, picking her way over the body of one sleeping gendarme who was stretched across the doorway to block the exit. She then discreetly boarded the next train for Moscow.

Exile could also be imposed as part of a court sentence, in which case it might be preceded by a period of penal servitude (*katorga*). In practice this usually involved confinement in a Siberian gaol, but not forced labour. Other, more feared political prisoners were put in solitary confinement in the cells of a fortress or prison, of which the Peter and Paul Fortress in St Petersburg and the Schlüsselburg Fortress, on an island on Lake Ladoga near the River Neva, were the most notorious. The Kiev Fortress was a common place of Nihilist detention; as was also the Kharkov Central Gaol, probably the most detested prison of all. One feature of imperial prisons in general was the remarkable ease with which political detainees could correspond with the outside world through bribed or sympathetic warders, whom they called pigeons. They also had an accepted code for communicating with each other by banging on the walls. And many were free to read and write, though the privilege was not automatic.

Given the choice, most prisoners would have preferred the climatically severe but easy-going conditions of Siberia to the rigours of a fortress or gaol in European Russia. It was easier to escape from Siberian detention or exile, though by no means easy to cross the borders of Siberia itself; the authorities relied on vast distances and primitive travel facilities to take the place of thick walls and careful supervision. But many revolutionaries did contrive Siberian escapes, including Bakunin at the beginning of the period studied here and Debogory-Mokriyevich towards the end.

One famous escape from European Russia was that of Prince Peter Kropotkin from the prison wing of the Nicholas Military Hospital in St Petersburg in 1876. While exercising in the yard, the anarchist Prince suddenly flung off his cumbrous green flannel prison dressing-gown and raced through the gates, pursued by a sentry and three soldiers. It was no sudden impulse, but the result of careful planning. Outside the hospital a friend was waiting in a fast carriage with a prizewinning trotter in the shafts, and pursuit was thwarted because accomplices had engaged all the cabs in the immediate neighbourhood. Kropotkin spent the afternoon lunching at his leisure in a private room at a fashionable restaurant while the hue and cry went on in the streets of St Petersburg around him. Shortly afterwards he escaped to England. Boarding a ship for Hull, he was much moved to see her flying the Union Jack: 'under which so many Russian, Italian, French and Hungarian refugees have found asylum.'[24]

8

The Hunting of the Tsar

Opponents of the Russian autocracy were constantly arguing about the degree of violence which might be desirable in assaulting the imperial State, and *Land and Freedom* soon split into two camps over this issue. In June 1879 attempts were made to patch up the differences at a conference, but the association had to be disbanded entirely later in the year. Its anti-terrorist members formed the group called *Black Repartition*, which was comparatively unimportant, while the more ruthlessly inclined set up a new party on avowedly terrorist principles: *People's Will.* On 26 August 1879, at a meeting held in a forest, *People's Will* formally condemned Alexander II to execution, a sentence which was carried out just over eighteen months later.

Alexander Mikhaylov, the first leader of the new group, set himself to establish a disciplined conspiratorial organization. *People's Will* thus fell into line with the ideas of the Russian *émigré* revolutionary Peter Tkachov. This former associate of Nechayev believed in an attack on the state by a centrally organized and disciplined revolutionary conspiracy, but was not himself an advocate of terrorism directed against prominent individuals such as formed the central policy of *People's Will.*

Henceforward *People's Will* assumed the monopoly in tsaricide. Alexander II had so far survived two assaults from his fellow-Russians, both by revolver, and had escaped each time through good luck and bad shooting. With these precedents to guide them, *People's Will* now rejected the revolver in favour of buried explosives which could be set off by delayed action or at some distance, offering the assassins a better chance of escape. Not that they set great store by their own skins; it was more in the interests of revolutionary prestige that they hoped to get away unscathed.

Logic seems to have played little part in the assassins' calculations. They had, and on the whole professed, no hope whatever of overthrowing the autocratic system and supplanting it with some other form of government, lacking as they did the resources even to attempt such a *coup*. The most they could expect as the immediate result of their efforts was to see the Tsarevich Alexander crowned in place of his father. But though the idea had somehow gained currency that the heir to the throne was a liberal, that impression was to prove sadly erroneous.

Another motive put forward by the Tsar's assassins was a wish for revenge on the man ultimately responsible for the execution of over a score of their comrades and for the imprisonment and exile of hundreds of others. The fact that the Tsar possessed, and regularly used, the power to revise penal sentences made it easy to regard him as personally to blame for the hangings; though there were also cases when he commuted a death sentence.

Another motive for killing the Tsar was sheer frustration. Most *People's Will* agents had been through the mill of trying to teach, heal or propagandize the peasantry, only to find their efforts all thwarted. Nor was there any apparent prospect of a constitution decisively limiting the autocrat's absolute power and giving Russian individuals the hope of exercising political influence. There was, it seemed, no useful form of non-violent activity open to them. And surely the assassination of a Tsar must at least bring about *some* change in a society where, as was innocently supposed, any innovation could only be for the better. The Nihilists were, alas, blissfully ignorant of the lengths to which tyranny can go, and would have been astonished to learn that other despots might arise in Russia and elsewhere beside whom Alexander II would seem as harmless as a babe in arms.

One also seems to sense beneath their gropings an addiction to destruction for its own sake, to the kind of Nihilism which is most akin to annihilation. High-minded sentiments, as commonly expressed by Nihilists, are not in themselves a proof of superior moral integrity, but may equally well be the cloak for political gangsterism. There have, after all, been few more consistently edifying pronouncements than those of Stalin's propagandists in the quarter-century of his supreme power, a period when self-righteous denunciation of 'Tsarist' atrocities went hand in hand with the infliction of atrocities on a scale many hundreds of times greater.

Though the missionary zeal and high-mindedness of Alexander II's killers do not absolve them from moral responsibility for their actions, the many manuscripts of trial proceedings, depositions and memoirs of the period give little colour to the idea that the typical Nihilist killed just for killing's sake or out of a belief, conscious or unconscious, in blind destruction. Human motives are in any case particularly difficult to unravel in a context of violence, and all one really knows about such deliberate killers as Sophia Perovsky and Andrey Zhelyabov is that they were deliberate killers. Yet it must be stressed that they, and many of their fellow-conspirators, did not embrace extreme violence suddenly, but were brought to it gradually after much experiment in other approaches. If it is hard to acclaim them as the shining heroes which some historians, Soviet and non-Soviet, have made of them, it is equally hard to see them as fiends in human shape. Had they, however, achieved power through some miracle, it seems likely that their brutality would have rivalled that of any nineteenth-century Tsar. No one after all kills with such fervour as those who claim that they are benefiting humanity, and one would be reluctant indeed to find one's personal fate in the hands of a Perovsky or Zhelyabov.

Winter and spring tended, as has been noted, to be the open season for hunting imperial functionaries, and to this rule the Emperor himself proved no exception. Before finally eliminating the sovereign on 1 March 1881, *People's Will* was to make six previous unsuccessful attempts, all involving explosives and all occurring in late 1879 and early 1880.

In the early winter of 1879 the Emperor was staying at Livadia, on the Crimean coast near Yalta. He was due to leave for St Petersburg in November, and the conspirators decided to strike at some point on the way. It was known that he would take one of two different routes: either by sea to Odessa and from there by rail; or else all the way by rail from Simferopol through Kharkov and Moscow. To cover all possibilities the conspirators decided to mine the line at three separate places. Mines had the excitement of novelty and the Russian railways were still in the first flush of youth, so the Nihilists could claim their tactics to be fully abreast of modern technology.

The first attempt to mine the track was made near Odessa, being organized by Vera Figner. It was decided to obtain the post of railway watchman somewhere near the town for one of the conspirators, and to use his hut as a base from which to tunnel under the line. With this in view Figner visited local officials disguised as a well-dressed society lady, a part which her upbringing well fitted her to play. She explained that an employee of hers had tuberculosis and needed an open-air job as railway watchman. Thus Michael Frolenko was installed in a suitable hut by the railway track about eight miles outside Odessa. But the weather turned bad and the Tsar, a poor sailor, decided to take the all-land route from Simferopol to St Petersburg instead of going through Odessa; so this plan had to be abandoned.

By leaving from Simferopol the Tsar was heading straight for a second ambush, which had been laid by Zhelyabov just outside Aleksandrovsk, then a small town, now much larger and renamed Zaporozhye. He had an elaborate cover-story to account for his presence here. Claiming to be a merchant from the north, he pretended to be planning a small tannery, for which purpose he leased land in the area. His days were spent beguiling local citizens with elaborate accounts of his business plans, while by night he and his confederates were burying two brass cylinders containing dynamite in the side of the railway embankment about four miles out of town. By 18 November all was in position, and word had reached Zhelyabov that the imperial party would travel in three trains, the Tsar himself being in the fourth coach of the second one.

As the coach reached the appropriate point on the embankment, an associate gave the command 'Fire!' and Zhelyabov pressed the switch. But for some reason the charge failed to explode. The conspirators had been blundering about in the dark and mud night after night, and were desperately tired; so it is not surprising that something went wrong. This affair has all the hallmarks of a *People's Will* operation: ruthless determination; enthusiastic play-acting by Zhelyabov as a self-styled merchant; inexperience in the handling of explosives; youthful ebullience; and sheer bad luck.

Meanwhile the three imperial trains continued to rumble northwards, and were due to reach Moscow on the following night, 19 November. The Tsar was now heading for a third ambush, and one which had caused the conspirators more sweat, toil and tears than the first two combined.

The main authority on the mining of the line in Moscow is the deposition made in prison by Alexander Mikhaylov, who was in charge of operations, but was arrested shortly afterwards. A small house had been bought for a thousand roubles in a Moscow suburb about fifty yards from the railway track and some two miles short of the Moscow–Kursk Railway Terminus. Sophia Perovsky and Leo Hartmann were installed under a suitable alias, and tunnelling began from the cellar, being mainly done by revolutionaries who were living elsewhere and came along to work in shifts.

This painful affair lasted several weeks. The gallery had to be run only three feet below the surface because the ground became water-logged if they tried to go below that level. Rain was always followed by serious flooding and the workings had to be laboriously cleared by bucket. They went under a side road, which began to show signs of subsidence as carts trundled over it; and it happened to be on the regular route taken by a heavy water wagon.

Work at the face was done by one man at a time, who, hunched awkwardly in the wet, sandy soil, shovelled out the earth by the light of a flickering candle and revetted with boards as he went along. Air was brought in by a simple ventilating system with inlet and outlet pipes, the draught being supplied by connexion with a stove-pipe inside the house. In case of alarm a bell could be sounded from an upstairs bedroom.

As is usual with secret tunnelling, the most difficult problem was disposing of the soil. Hauled out by rope on a sheet of metal, the sodden earth was stowed in spare rooms or privily scattered in the yard at night. Neighbours did not notice this, but grew inquisitive, partly because so much food seemed to be going into the house; Perovsky had to satisfy their curiosity by inventing a cat with a legendary appetite. Like many Nihilists, she had learnt to be a good character actress.

Each foot of advance towards the railway embankment brought more difficulties and dangers. The more nearly they approached the line, the more menacing were the thunderous drummings and deafening vibrations of each passing train. 'You could clearly hear the wheels leaping from one rail to another in staccato jerks,' Mikhaylov later told the authorities.[25] The tunneller at the face knew that the next train might start an avalanche which would bury him alive. It was there, Mikhaylov said, that he looked into the cold eyes of death, but was not afraid.

According to available intelligence the Tsar would still be travelling in the second train of a convoy of three, and in the fourth coach. Perovsky kept watch and gave the agreed signal at the critical moment, whereupon Hartmann duly fired the charge and a loud bang followed, showing that there had been no technical hitch on this occasion. But there had been a hitch of another kind. The Tsar had, after all, decided to travel in the first train instead of the second, and had already arrived safely at the terminus. The only casualty was a consignment of jam from his Crimean estates, carried in the crucial fourth coach which was derailed and thrown on its side. The conspirators escaped immediate detection and Hartmann found refuge in France.

At Odessa the plotters had not even put the dynamite in position; at Aleksandrovsk they had placed charges but failed to detonate them; now at Moscow they had detonated a charge without killing anyone, but they did at least seem to be getting the range of their target. Their next attempt, the celebrated explosion under the Tsar's dining-room in the Winter Palace, marked a still closer approach.

This attempt was the work of Stephen Khalturin, a somewhat exceptional figure among Russian revolutionaries, since he was a working man. It was as a carpenter, with a good record of employment on the imperial yacht, that he obtained a job in the Winter Palace itself in the autumn of 1879. Studying the layout, he found that his own quarters in the cellar were just below a guardroom which was in turn directly below the Tsar's private dining-room. The Tsar had usually started his dinner by six o'clock in the evening, and if enough explosive could be detonated in the cellar, he was sure to be killed. As for the unfortunate soldiers in between, their fate would naturally be a matter for regret.

Slowly, over the months, Khalturin smuggled into the Palace small quantities of dynamite with which he was regularly supplied by accomplices belonging to *People's Will*. He kept his stocks under his pillow until the fumes began to give him headaches, then stored them in the trunk which he kept under his bed. There were, as usual, various hitches, including one without precedent: a resident corporal of gendarmes decided that Khalturin would make a suitable son-in-law and therefore paid him unwelcome attention. But on the evening of 5 February all was ready and Khalturin set off his delayed-action fuse, left the Palace and was in the square outside when, at twenty minutes past six, a great explosion shook the area. The palace lights went out and the conspirators had their moment of triumph.

But the Emperor's luck still held. That evening, as it happened, he had been detained for an unusually long time giving audience to a visiting notable. When the bomb went off, he had not yet reached the dining-room, and because of this he escaped injury. Others were less lucky; eleven persons were killed and over fifty injured, mostly soldiers.

People's Will had drawn blood.

In the late spring of 1880 two further ambushes were laid for the monarch, this time on his journey south from St Petersburg to the Crimea.

The first trap was set in St Petersburg itself, under the Kamenny Bridge on the Catherine Canal, which the Tsar was to cross on his way to the railway station, this affair being organized by Zhelyabov. Nearly a hundredweight of dynamite was lowered into the canal, in a waterproof wrapping, and wires were connected and taken to a raft. Here Zhelyabov kept an appointed rendezvous with an accomplice who frustrated the plot by arriving late; Russian terrorists, it was reflected, could not afford to indulge in the national vice of unpunctuality.

Meanwhile more tunnelling had been under way in Odessa, to mine a street along which the Emperor was to pass on his way to the harbour from the railway station. This affair was managed by Figner and Perovsky, a guarantee that it would be prosecuted energetically. They started a grocery shop on a suitable site and digging began, but the plan had to be abandoned owing to a change in the Emperor's travelling arrangements.

The strains of revolutionary activity make it a great revealer of character, but there are also factors operating in the opposite direction. Since assassination plans have to be carefully concealed at the time, many terrorists take their secrets with them to the grave. Another difficulty is the tendency of revolutionaries, in their memoirs at least, to form a mutual admiration society. One may read in A's memoirs about the brave, noble and self-sacrificing qualities of B – only to find, in B's memoirs, almost identical dithyrambs about A. There are also examples of the opposite tendency, the lapsed Nihilist Tikhomirov being particularly unkind about his former colleagues, as was Nicholas Uspensky writing about Nihilists of the previous decade. Fortunately, however, such a wealth of varied information is available that it is often possible to discount bias in both directions.

Three personalities stand out: they were all involved in the final and successful assault on the monarch.

Andrey Zhelyabov, who took over as leader of *People's Will* after Alexander Mikhaylov's arrest, was born a serf, and became an enemy of imperial society early in life because of a traumatic experience suffered as a child: an aunt of whom he was very fond was raped by the local landlord, who sent his bailiff to drag her from the hut where the boy was living with his grandparents. Zhelyabov witnessed this abduction and the episode made him decide to kill the landlord when he grew up, a plan destined to be swallowed up in greater ambitions. He had a long career as an active revolutionary, going over in the middle of 1879 to the policy of terrorism by becoming a founder-member of *People's Will*. He was gay, dynamic and restless. Unlike some Nihilists, he by no means regarded every woman as a sister, but combined with his prowess as lover an unusually strong revolutionary death-wish. It was he who planned the successful assassination, only to be arrested two days before it took place, so that he had no hand in the action itself; the original plan, incidentally, had included a provision that he was to finish the Tsar off with a dagger if all else failed. When he heard, in prison, of the Tsar's death, Zhelyabov hastened to implicate himself, and demanded outright to be hanged, saying that it would be unfair to him to give him a lesser sentence.

Sophia Perovsky lived with Zhelyabov as his wife towards the end. When he was arrested she took over as tactical leader, and her performance in the field showed her to be well-trained in the battle-drill of assassination and possessed of a true killer instinct. She was also a charming and attractive young woman; at least there are so many contemporary witnesses to this effect, including a testimonial from the police, that it would probably be misleading as well as ungallant to give weight to the forbidding and unfeminine impression made by many of her photographs. Attractive or not, Perovsky was a bossy girl. She was once engaged to be married to Tikhomirov, before she turned him down, only to be repaid later by appearing in his memoirs as a conceited, tyrannical person who liked power and surrounded herself with nonentities and mediocrities. Tikhomirov is not the best of witnesses, and the general impression of Sophia is less extreme, but shows her as a young woman with a strong will and a low opinion of masculine competence. As has been well said, she 'would have made an excellent governess'.[26] Instead of this she became the first woman in Russia to be executed for a political offence.

Vera Figner was another leading terrorist intimately involved in hunting the Tsar, after which she eluded arrest for two years. She became a living legend to lesser Nihilists as the only important surviving leader of *People's Will* to stay in Russia and remain active after 1881. One minor figure in the movement describes her reputation as a super-revolutionary renowned for her beauty and elegance (evidence in her case not belied by photographs), as well as for breeding, intelligence and ability to appear in any society including the most aristocratic.[27]

She was arrested in 1883, and survived twenty-two years in Schlüsselburg Fortress, and also three Russian revolutions, as well as the First and part of the Second World War. She was much in demand to write introductions to the numerous Nihilist memoirs which began to flood the presses as soon as it became possible to print them. These include the reminiscences of the defector Tikhomirov, who gets short shrift from this grand old lady of Russian terrorism.

The unsuccessful operations at the Kamenny Bridge and in Odessa were followed by a nine-month lull in assaults on the Emperor. But the terrorists were not marking time. Having failed to kill the sovereign in his palace or on annual journeyings between St Petersburg and the Crimea, they now decided to attack on the streets of St Petersburg itself, using the time-honoured device of tunnelling and mine-laying which had never so far succeeded. But as criminals are said to leave the signature of individual technique on murders or burglaries, so *People's Will* was addicted to shovel and dynamite. This technique had been several times frustrated by unexpected variations in travelling arrangements, but if some regular pattern

top Alexander II (1818–81), the Nihilists' most distinguished victim

above The Nihilist attempt to blow up the imperial train near Moscow, 1 December 1879

After the attempt to blow up the Winter Palace on 5 February 1880

The arrival of the first fire-engine after the attempt to blow up the Winter Palace

1 March 1881. A moment before the first explosion on the Catherine Quay

1 March 1881. The first explosion

above opposite 1 March 1881. After the explosion of the second bomb

below opposite Another artist's impression of the same

The trial of the six persons concerned in the assassination of the Tsar. The prisoners (seated top right, reading from left to right): Rysakov, Timothy Mikhaylov, Jessie Helfmann, Kibalchich, Sophia Perovsky, Zhelyabov

opposite The condemned prisoners

THE ILLUSTRATED LONDON NEWS,

REGISTERED AT THE GENERAL POST-OFFICE FOR TRANSMISSION ABROAD.

No. 2188.—VOL. LXXVIII. SATURDAY, APRIL 23, 1881. TWO WHOLE SHEETS | SIXPENCE. By Post, 6½d.

Alexander II after death

The execution in 1882 of Nicholas Sukhanov, a former naval officer, who took part in the preparations for the assassination of Alexander II

could now be found in the Emperor's movements within the capital, the risk of last-minute changes of plan might be minimized.

From late 1880 onwards the monarch was discreetly stalked and watched on the streets of his capital by agents of *People's Will*. Sunday, they found, was the most promising day of the week, as the day on which he kept closest to routine, driving late in the morning a distance of about a mile from his Winter Palace to the Mikhaylov Manège, a cavalry parade ground. Here he would briefly review his troops and then return. He would travel each way in his carriage, convoyed by mounted Cossacks and followed by sleighs containing police and military officers. The normal route from the Winter Palace took this cavalcade down the Nevsky Prospekt for a few hundred yards, after which it would turn left up Malaya Sadovaya Street.

It was on the corner of this street that the assassins decided to strike. They rented basement premises, set up a cheese shop with two conspirators in charge under the alias of Mr and Mrs Kobozev, and began digging. This time the tunnel was to be only fifteen feet long, so there was hope of avoiding the ordeals associated with the affair of the Kursk–Moscow railway line over a year earlier; that tunnel, it may be remembered, had been about ten times as long. But the excavation of the Malaya Sadovaya had its moments. At one point the tunnellers broke into a sewer and were nearly choked. Besides, the 'Kobozevs' kept attracting suspicion because they forgot to behave like serious cheese-vendors. 'Mrs Kobozev', for instance, was always smoking cigarettes: sound Nihilist practice, but not a habit usual among Russian shopkeepers' wives at this date. And then the premises were suddenly raided, almost at the last minute, by an inspecting party under a General who through some miracle of inattention failed to notice or interpret the piles of wet earth roughly covered over with straw and coke.

Disaster struck when Zhelyabov, leader of the whole enterprise, was arrested on 27 February. But it was decided to proceed with the attack, scheduled for 1 March, with Perovsky as commander in the field. As a reserve plan it had been decided to arm four young men with home-made hand-grenades and station them in the Malaya Sadovaya. They were to wait for the mine to explode and then rush up to finish the Tsar off if necessary. They were also to hold themselves ready, if so directed, to stage an alternative ambush at the last moment by going to prearranged stations on the Catherine Quay.

This lay on a different route which the Tsar sometimes used and which did not take him along Malaya Sadovaya Street.

The night of 28 February to 1 March was spent in Figner's conspiratorial apartment laboriously constructing, under the supervision of the explosives expert Kibalchich, four cumbrous hand-grenades weighing about five pounds each. Success could only be guaranteed within a radius of about a yard, so it was certain that whoever threw one would be caught, assuming that he did not perish in the explosion. But there was an exalted (or hysterical) mood of self-sacrifice among *People's Will* by now. Many members of the Party had written off their own lives, and in any case their main hopes were pinned on the street mine.

At 12.55 p.m. on Sunday, 1 March, the Tsar duly drove out through the wooden barricades at the exit from the Winter Palace. He wore a dark blue cloak and a helmet with a white plume. The imperial coachman was resplendent in scarlet and there was a Cossack bodyguard on the box. In front, to the sides and behind rode Cossacks in their scarlet Circassian coats, mounted on black horses. Two sleighs, conveying the chief of police and other uniformed functionaries, rode closely behind. The Tsar gave the order to drive to the Mikhaylov Parade Ground; but by the less common, northerly route along the Catherine Quay, which would not take him over the Malaya Sadovaya. Once again a Nihilist plot seemed to have gone awry.

The question of the moment was: would he return by the Malaya Sadovaya? It began to seem unlikely when a look-out reported that he had already left the Parade Ground and gone a short distance to pay a call (as was his occasional custom) on his cousin, the Grand Duchess Catherine, whose residence was the Mikhaylov Palace on the north side of Engineer Street.

This made it likely that the Tsar would now return by the route taken on his outward journey just over an hour earlier. If so the Malaya Sadovaya must be written off, but there was still time to switch the four bombardiers to the Catherine Quay. Perovsky gave an agreed signal (blowing her nose), at which they went to their alternative stations, while she crossed the canal and stood at a point where she could see down Engineer Street. On sighting the imperial cavalcade, she alerted the four by another signal of the handkerchief. Everything now depended on them and, as has already been described, two bombs were thrown: the first narrowly missed the Tsar, who walked back to the scene of the explosion only to be caught by the second. The dying sovereign was removed to his palace and at three fifty-five the population of the imperial capital saw the flag on the Winter Palace lowered.

Alexander II was dead and the Russian revolutionary movement now had to reckon with Alexander III, a more daunting experience altogether.

For their part in assassinating the Emperor five persons went to the scaffold on 3 April 1881. Everything was done to make this barbaric ceremony a memorable cautionary pageant for the crowds of people in the streets of St Petersburg who watched the condemned criminals taken in solemn procession from the Remand Prison, and for the huge throng which witnessed the act of execution in Semyonov Square.

Inside the prison early on this sunny morning the condemned were arrayed in the prescribed black clothes and strapped in position on two special tumbrils: unsprung carts with platforms fourteen foot high mounted on them. Their wrists and ankles were fettered, they had their backs to the horses, and each bore on his chest a placard with the word TSARICIDE in white letters on a black ground.

The leading tumbril conveyed Zhelyabov himself. By his side was Nicholas Rysakov, who had opened the attack on the Catherine Quay: the last courageous act of his life. In custody he turned traitor, and for a whole month had been confessing all he knew about his comrades in the hope of saving his skin. Thus the others were in a sense Rysakov's victims, just as he was theirs. As a youth of nineteen he had fallen under the spell of Zhelyabov's dominant personality, only to shake off the influence when it was too late. Now, on his last day on earth, he had become an abject, cringing wreck whom his four condemned associates treated with open contempt.

The second tumbril carried Sophia Perovsky. Strapped on either side of her were Kibalchich, the explosives expert, and Timothy Mikhaylov, who had been a member of the bomb-throwing squad on 1 March. It appears that he took fright then and failed to carry out his role, but he now went to meet his death with courage.

Massed troops and a crowd of eighty thousand sightseers, together with representatives of the diplomatic corps and foreign press, awaited the cortège in Semyonov Square, in the centre of which a huge scaffold some twenty feet high had been erected. The ceremonies included the chaining of the five assassins to pillars of shame and the lengthy reading of the court's sentence, with drum rolls in the intervals to prevent any of the condemned marring the proceedings with a last-minute message of defiance or political testament. Five Orthodox priests, robed in funereal chasubles, offered the last rites of the church, which were accepted or rejected in varying degree, though all kissed the Cross. Behind the scaffold five coffins had been discreetly stacked.

Such lavish panoply and elaborate preparations were often, in Russia, the prelude to that most Russian of institutions – the public *skandal* – and the present occasion was no exception. The red-shirted hangman prepared his ropes and the victims were arrayed in the special funeral shrouds used on these occasions; white, hooded affairs with a slit at the throat for the noose, they resembled the robes of the Ku Klux Klan.

Even at its best a Russian hanging was no mercy killing. There was no trap or drop. With a noose round his neck, the victim stood on a low stand which was simply kicked or shoved away, after which he expired in a slow writhing agony of strangulation.

These horrors were now compounded, not for the first time in the history of Russian public hangings, by the incompetence of an executioner who needed Dutch courage to perform his function and was accustomed to present the authorities with a bill for vodka consumed in the course of duty. Timothy Mikhaylov had to be hanged three times because the noose slipped and his heavy carcase began to pull the metal ring, to which the rope was attached, out of the cross-beam. There were other unsavoury details into which it is not necessary to enter, except to mention that an army medical officer, officially present to witness proceedings, was at one point moved to protest; whereupon the drunken hangman rounded and cursed him.

It was to observe such bungling that a vast crowd and some ten thousand troops had assembled. Not for the first or last time the imperial authorities lost face with the public, and the comment was to be heard that 'we Russians can't even hang a man properly'.

While the other four victims met death with dignity, the unhappy

Rysakov (whom they studiously ignored during last-minute embraces) clung to life till the last moment, desperately kicking to keep a grip with his feet on the foot-stand when the executioner pushed it away. But life was eventually extinct in all five terrorists, and with it the life of the Nihilist movement as it had been known in the reign of its most illustrious victim.

References

1 Vladimir Debogory-Mokriyevich, *Vospominaniya* (St Petersburg, 1906), p. 367.
2 *Ibid.*, p. 35.
3 *Ibid.*, p. 109.
4 Quoted in Franco Venturi, *Roots of Revolution* (London, 1960), p. 227.
5 N. V. Shelgunov, *Vospominaniya* (Moscow-Petrograd, 1923), p. 219.
6 Korney Chukovsky, *Lyudi i knigi* (Moscow, 1960), p. 163.
7 Nestor Kotlyarevsky, *Kanun osvobozhdeniya* (Petrograd, 1916), p. 445.
8 Shelgunov, *op. cit.*, p. 121.
9 T. A. Bogdanovich, *Lyubov lyudey shestidesyatykh godov* (Leningrad, 1929), pp. 283 and 380.
10 I. S. Turgenev, *Sobraniye sochineny* (Moscow, 1954–58), vol. x, p. 636.
11 Charles A. Moser, *Antinihilism in the Russian Novel of the 1860s* (The Hague, 1964).
12 *Ibid.*, p. 85.
13 David Footman, *Red Prelude* (London, 1944), p. 31.
14 Venturi, *op. cit.*, p. 373.
15 See E. H. Carr, *The Romantic Exiles* (Harmondsworth, 1949), p. 340.
16 Stepnyak (Sergey Kravchinsky), *Podpolnaya Rossiya* (St Petersburg, 1906), p. 12.
17 Vera Figner, *Zapechatlyonny trud* (Moscow, 1964), p. 161.
18 Debogory-Mokriyevich, *op. cit.*, p. 237.
19 Figner, *op. cit.*, p. 140.
20 Leo Tikhomirov, *Vospominaniya* (Moscow-Leningrad, 1927), pp. 106–7.
21 *Ibid.*, p. 118.
22 Footman, *op. cit.*, p. 93.
23 Leo Deutsch, *Sixteen Years in Siberia* (London, 1903), pp. 287–8.

24 P. A. Kropotkin, *Zapiski revolyutsionera* (Moscow–Leningrad, 1933), p. 244.
25 A. P. Pribyleva-Korba and V. N. Figner, *A. D. Mikhaylov* (Moscow–Leningrad, 1925), p. 140.
26 Footman, *op. cit.*, p. 81.
27 I. I. Popov, *Minuvsheye i perezhitoye* (*Academia*, 1933), p. 108.

Note on the word 'Nihilist'

The more one studies the word Nihilist, the more shades of meaning it seems to have, especially as some authorities apparently employ it with several different senses within the confines of a single work. So it seems worth stressing that, unless otherwise qualified, the word has been used in this book exactly in accordance with the subtitle: as an equivalent for 'Russian radicals and revolutionaries in the reign of Alexander II (1855–81)'.

There is no space here to argue the case for adopting this definition, except to say that it accords with general Western European usage in the period studied – as also with Russian usage during the period, apart from that of the Nihilists themselves; on the whole, as has been shown, they preferred to be called by some other name which they considered more ennobling, such as Populists, revolutionaries or – somewhat ingenuously – 'honest men'. Our definition of Nihilist also accords with that given in the *Shorter Oxford English Dictionary*: 'a member of a Russian revolutionary party professing extreme antisocial principles'. It must be admitted that the extent to which Nihilist principles are extremely 'antisocial' is open to argument, though the reader of this book will have no difficulty in detecting that the author is in broad agreement with the dictionary here.

Some authorities would find fault with the solution adopted and claim that the term Nihilist should be used more narrowly, to describe various categories of person who form only part of the subject-matter treated here: those young Russians who anticipated the twentieth-century 'beatniks' by a hundred years in hair-style and general 'bloody-mindedness'; or the followers of Dmitry Pisarev; or Russian radicals and revolutionaries in the earlier part of our period only: the 'Sixties' (a further complication being that according to some Russian social historians the 'Sixties' began in 1855 and ended in 1866, or even 1861). Then again, the word may also have a much wider connotation than that with which it is used here: to describe those – whether in Russia or anywhere else on the globe – who reject current religious beliefs or moral principles; or who carry philosophical scepticism to the extreme point of denying that anything exists at all. Moreover, as emerges from our text, these various meanings are not independent of one another, but overlap and interact.

The situation is further bedevilled by the claims of other terms of somewhat similar scope, used to describe various kinds of person opposed to the policies and institutions of imperial Russia. Besides radicals, revolutionaries, Populists and 'honest men', these also include Jacobins, leftists, terrorists, socialists, progressives, anarchists, Men of the Sixties, New People, liberals, 'mixed-rankers', seminarists, reds, students, the intelligentsia and the freedom movement. These terms overlap with each other and with Nihilism. And in common with Nihilism they all have a variety of possible meanings and applications of their own, while some carry derogatory and others approving overtones, each varying in intensity with the outlook of the individual user.

Bibliographical Note and Suggestions for Further Reading

Nihilist thought has been treated much more exhaustively in English than has Nihilist action. The most useful single study covering the subject as a whole is Franco Venturi's *Il populismo russo*, translated into English as *Roots of Revolution* (London, 1960). E. Lampert's *Sons against Fathers* (Oxford, 1965) gives a useful study of Chernyshevsky, Dobrolyubov and Pisarev. S. V. Utechin's *Russian Political Thought* (New York, 1964) is an excellent and admirably clear introduction to an involved subject.

For a valuable study more concentrated on narrative than on analysis of ideas, see David Footman's *Red Prelude: A Life of A. I. Zhelyabov* (London, 1944).

Though mainly devoted to a single aspect of the subject only, Charles A. Moser's *Antinihilism in the Russian Novel of the 1860s* (The Hague, 1964) contains one of the ablest brief descriptions of the Nihilist movement. Reference may also be made to an older work, Thomas G. Masaryk's *The Spirit of Russia*, 2 vols. (London, 1955) and to A. Coquart's *Dmitri Pisarev (1840–1868) et l'Idéologie du nihilisme russe* (Paris, 1946).

All these works contain much useful bibliographical information.

Index